The kingdom has come

LUKE 1 – 12

by Mike McKinley

thegood**book**
COMPANY

Luke 1-12 For You

If you are reading *Luke 1–12 For You* alongside this Good Book Guide, here is how the studies in this booklet link to the chapters of *Luke 1–12 For You*:

Study One → Ch 1
Study Two → Ch 2-3
Study Three → Ch 3-4
Study Four → Ch 5-6

Study Five → Ch 7
Study Six → Ch 8-10
Study Seven → Ch 10-11
Study Eight → Ch 12

Find out more about *Luke 1–12 For You* at:
www.thegoodbook.com/for-you

The kingdom has come
The Good Book Guide to Luke 1 – 12
© Michael McKinley/The Good Book Company, 2016. Reprinted 2019.
Series Consultants: Tim Chester, Tim Thornborough,
                    Anne Woodcock, Carl Laferton

The Good Book Company
Tel: (US): 866 244 2165
Tel (UK): 0333 123 0880
Email (US): info@thegoodbook.com
Email (UK): info@thegoodbook.co.uk

Websites
North America: www.thegoodbook.com
UK: www.thegoodbook.co.uk
Australia: www.thegoodbook.com.au
New Zealand: www.thegoodbook.co.nz

ISBN: 9781784980160

Printed in Turkey

CONTENTS

Introduction: Good Book Guides

Every Bible-study group is different—yours may take place in a church building, in a home or in a cafe, on a train, over a leisurely mid-morning coffee or squashed into a 30-minute lunch break. Your group may include new Christians, mature Christians, non-Christians, moms and tots, students, businessmen or teens. That's why we've designed these *Good Book Guides* to be flexible for use in many different situations.

Our aim in each session is to uncover the meaning of a passage, and see how it fits into the "big picture" of the Bible. But that can never be the end. We also need to appropriately apply what we have discovered to our lives. Let's take a look at what is included:

⊕ **Talkabout:** Most groups need to "break the ice" at the beginning of a session, and here's the question that will do that. It's designed to get people talking around a subject that will be covered in the course of the Bible study.

⊡ **Investigate:** The Bible text for each session is broken up into manageable chunks, with questions that aim to help you understand what the passage is about. The **Leader's Guide** contains **guidance for questions**, and sometimes ⊗ additional "follow-up" questions.

⊡ **Explore more (optional):** These questions will help you connect what you have learned to other parts of the Bible, so you can begin to fit it all together like a jig-saw; or occasionally look at a part of the passage that's not dealt with in detail in the main study.

⊡ **Apply:** As you go through a Bible study, you'll keep coming across **apply** sections. These are questions to get the group discussing what the Bible teaching means in practice for you and your church. ⊡ **Getting personal** is an opportunity for you to think, plan and pray about the changes that you personally may need to make as a result of what you have learned.

⊡ **Pray:** We want to encourage prayer that is rooted in God's word—in line with his concerns, purposes and promises. So each session ends with an opportunity to review the truths and challenges highlighted by the Bible study, and turn them into prayers of request and thanksgiving.

The **Leader's Guide** and introduction provide historical background information, explanations of the Bible texts for each session, ideas for **optional extra** activities, and guidance on how best to help people uncover the truths of God's word.

Why study Luke?

The Gospel of Luke was written to give Christians certainty. That alone makes it a priceless part of Scripture, and a must-read for you and me.

But what *are* those things about which we are supposed to have certainty?

First, Luke offers us certainty about *who Jesus is*—he is the fulfillment of all God's promises throughout history. Luke shows us that the life and death and resurrection of Jesus are all a part of a definite plan that God has revealed in the Old Testament and is now unfolding for the salvation of his people. We will listen in on Jesus standing up in his hometown synagogue, reading the Old Testament, and announcing that, "Today this scripture is fulfilled in your hearing" (4 v 21). God had promised to send a King to rule and rescue his people—and in Jesus, he kept his promise.

Second, Luke offers us certainty about *who Jesus came for*. Again and again, we will see that Jesus is not limited to the people that were valued and honored in the society of that day. In fact, we will be surprised by who it is who finds a home in the kingdom that Jesus came to bring; and by what kind of person walks away from him, confused and even offended by him.

So third, Luke offers us certainty about *what Jesus' kingdom is like*. Jesus came to "proclaim the good news of the kingdom of God"—it was, he said, "why I was sent" (Luke 4 v 43). We'll discover through what he says and does that his kingdom is a place of justice, of forgiveness, of trust and compassion and blessing and commitment. It's why to welcome the King is to discover real joy—the Gospel of Luke uses the words "joy" and "rejoice" more than any other book of the New Testament.

In these eight studies you'll see that the kingdom really has come because the King really did come. And you'll appreciate what it means to be part of that kingdom, and how its citizens live and feel as they follow the One in whom all of God's promises are kept.

Note: Some of the studies in this book cover large sections of Luke. Occasionally, you'll be asked to read a short passage, with a longer passage following in brackets. If you want to read all of Luke 1 – 12 as a group, then read the passages given in the parentheses.

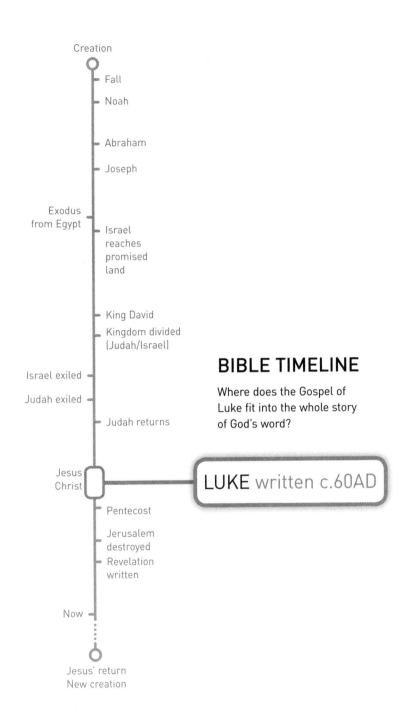

Creation

Fall

Noah

Abraham

Joseph

Exodus
from Egypt

Israel
reaches
promised
land

King David

Kingdom divided
(Judah/Israel)

Israel exiled

Judah exiled

Judah returns

BIBLE TIMELINE

Where does the Gospel of
Luke fit into the whole story
of God's word?

Jesus
Christ

LUKE written c.60AD

Pentecost

Jerusalem
destroyed

Revelation
written

Now

Jesus' return
New creation

1

Luke 1 v 1 – 2 v 40
NOTHING IS IMPOSSIBLE

⊕ talkabout

1. Whose promises do you most trust, and why? Whose promises do you least trust, and why?

⊕ investigate

> **Read Luke 1 v 1-4**

2. Why is Luke writing (v 4)? How do verses 1-3 give us confidence in what he is writing?

DICTIONARY

Fulfilled (v 1): brought about; completed.

> **Read Luke 1 v 26-56 (1 v 5-80)**

The angel tells Mary about two pregnancies—her own (v 31), and that of her relative Elizabeth (v 36).

3. Why are both impossible?

DICTIONARY

Jacob (v 33): the ancestor of every member of Israel.
Glorifies (v 46): recognizes the brilliance of.
Abraham (v 55): Jacob's grandfather.

• Why does Mary know they will happen (v 37-38)?

4. What is God like, according to Mary's "song" in verses 46-55?

• Mary's son is "the Son of the Most High," whose "kingdom will never end" (v 32-33). How does her song make us excited about her child's birth?

5. Track Mary's responses to what is going on in v 29-30, 38, 46-47. What does she show us about what true faith looks like?

⊟ **apply**

6. Why, and when, do we find it hard to live with Mary-like faith?

⊡ getting personal

God can do what he says he will do. You can live each day confident
that God will keep all of the promises he has made to his people,
no matter how far removed they might seem from your daily
circumstances and inner feelings.

How are you finding that hardest right now?

How will you use Luke 1 to help you?

What would it look like to rejoice in God, your Savior, instead of
worrying or fearing?

⊍ investigate

> **Read Luke 2 v 1-20**

⊡ explore more

optional

Why did Mary and Joseph travel to Bethlehem (v 1-5)?

In verse 4, Luke twice mentions King David. Bethlehem was his
hometown, and Joseph was from his line.

> **Read 2 Samuel 7 v 11b-16 and Micah 5 v 2-4**

Why is Bethlehem significant? Who would be born there?

*How does this show that Augustus is not quite as powerful as it
appeared, and that his empire is not quite as important as it seemed?*

The lowly circumstances of Jesus' birth show us that God's kingdom will
come in ways that surprise and subvert our expectations about what
true greatness and power look like—something we will see repeatedly
as we walk through the Gospel of Luke.

7.   On the night that Mary has her baby (v 6-7), what does an angel tell some
shepherds nearby about who that baby is (v 10-12)?

8. What responses to God's work that night do we see here?

▶ **Read Luke 2 v 21-40**

9. What have Simeon and Anna been waiting for (v 25-26, 36-38)?

> **DICTIONARY**
>
> **Law of Moses/Law of the Lord (v 22,23):** the way God told his people to live before the coming of his Messiah.
> **Righteous (v 25):** here, meaning seeking to live God's way.
> **Consolation of Israel (v 25):** the time when Israel would be rescued and restored, as promised by God in the Old Testament.
> **Gentiles (v 32):** non-Jews.
> **Redemption (v 38):** freedom, bought at a cost.

• Both realize that, in the baby Jesus, they are looking at the end of their time of waiting. What does this tell us about what this baby has been born to do?

10. What does Simeon tell Mary in verses 34-35?

• How is this a jarring note amid all the joy surrounding Jesus' birth? What do you think it is talking about?

11. Imagine you had never heard of Jesus or read the Bible, and you had picked up Luke's Gospel and reached 2 v 40. What would you think about:

- who this baby is?
- what he has come to do?

⤷ apply

12. What reactions of people who truly realize who Jesus is has Luke shown us? How would these look in our lives today?

⊡ getting personal

Think back to your answers to the Getting Personal after Question Six. How do the events of Luke 2 give you greater cause to rejoice in God in areas where you struggle to believe his promises?

⬆ pray

Thank God that "no matter how many promises God has made, they are 'Yes' in Christ" (2 Corinthians 1 v 20). Then use your answers to Question Twelve to fuel your requests to God.

2
Luke 2 v 41 – 4 v 13
WALKING IN OUR SHOES

The story so far

God worked to keep his impossible-seeming promises through sending his Son, Jesus, to be his promised King. This is good news of great joy!

⊕ talkabout

1. Why do people get so joyful and/or so sad about the fortunes of the sporting teams they support?

⊕ investigate

▶ Read Luke 3 v 1-22 (2 v 41 – 3 v 22)

2. What was baptism by John, Jesus' relative, "for" (that is, a sign of—v 3)?

> **DICTIONARY**
>
> **Repentance (v 3):** turning away from sinning and toward the Lord in obedience.
> **Wrath (v 7):** God's settled anger at humanity's sin.
> **Winnowing fork (v 17):** used by farmers to separate the wheat (the good part of the plant) from the chaff (which was thrown away or burned).

Baptism was (and is) an act with layers of deep symbolic significance, and one of the things that it represents is identification with or inclusion in something. So Paul can speak of the Israelites being baptized "into Moses" (1 Corinthians 10 v 2) and Christians being baptized "into one body" (1 Corinthians 12 v 13, ESV) and "into Christ" (Romans 6 v 3; Galatians 3 v 27). To be baptized is to make a statement about your loyalty, allegiance, and identity.

3. So when Jesus comes to be baptized (v 21), what kind of people is he identifying with?

4. What is different, and unique, about Jesus' baptism (v 21-22)?

Jesus was baptized to show that he had come to identify with sinners—so that sinners could be identified with him.

5. Reading the Father's verdict on Jesus in verse 22, why is this brilliant news for us?

⊡ **apply**

6. What difference does sharing in Jesus' standing before God make when:
  • we worry about what others think of us?

  • we become aware of our failings?

• we fulfill a great dream or achieve a success?

⊡ getting personal

If you are united to Christ through faith, the love and pleasure that God has for his Son is extended to you as well.

How does this fact make you feel?

When in your life and circumstances do you particularly need to call this to mind?

⊻ investigate

❯ Read Luke 4 v 1-13

7. Who is doing battle in the wilderness (v 1-2)?

⊡ explore more

optional

We have already seen that Jesus is God's Son (3 v 22).

❯ Read Luke 3 v 23-38

Who else is described as "the son of God" (v 38)?

Adam, the son of God and the image of God (Genesis 1 v 26-27), was created to represent God to the world.

❯ Read Genesis 3 v 1-19

What did he do instead, and with what results?

Wonderfully, God did not abandon the project of creating a race of image-bearers for his glory. He called the nation of Israel to be "my son" (Exodus 4 v 22-23) and rescued them from slavery, calling them to represent him to the world (Leviticus 19 v 1-2).

> ▶ **Read Numbers 13 v 1-3; 13 v 26 – 14 v 4; 14 v 26-35**

When they were in the wilderness, how did the "son" treat his Father?

So don't miss what is at stake in the temptation of Jesus. Adam, the son of God, was tempted by Satan and chose not to obey the word of the Lord. Israel was tested in the wilderness and descended into sinful grumbling and disbelief of God's promises. Now in Luke 4, will the second Adam succeed where the first one failed? Will the new Israel be faithful where the old one rebelled?

8. Think about what kind of life Satan is offering Jesus with each temptation.

• Why would each offer have been extremely tempting?

9. Each time, Jesus stands firm and obeys his Father. What does the devil do next (v 13)?

The skirmishes would continue until the cross, when Jesus appeared defeated. But in an irony that has perhaps become too familiar for us to fully appreciate, it was in that moment of "defeat" that Jesus delivered the decisive blow to his enemy. The battle that raged in the wilderness here would ultimately be won on the cross of Calvary.

⊡ apply

Remember that in baptism, Jesus was identifying with sinful people so that sinful people could be identified with him.

10. How does that make his obedience in the wilderness precious for us?

11. What does the experience of Jesus in the wilderness teach us:
- most importantly, about how we can respond when we give in to temptation?

- about how we go about resisting temptation?

⊡ getting personal

Is there a sin you are carrying about which Satan has convinced you that you cannot be forgiven? What difference will it make if you remember that it is Jesus' obedience, and not your disobedience, that God "sees"?

Is there a temptation you keep giving in to, that Satan has convinced you does not matter or cannot be resisted? How has Jesus' baptism and wilderness experience motivated you to obey instead of sinning?

⊓ **pray**

Spend time thanking God for sending his Son to identify with you, so that you might be identified with him. Praise Jesus for resisting temptation perfectly throughout his life, and for all that that means for you.

Share the temptations you find yourself battling against most commonly, and giving in to most frequently. Pray for one another, that you would rely on the salvation of Jesus and follow the example of Jesus.

3 Luke 4 v 14 – 5 v 39
INTO THE KINGDOM

The story so far

God worked to keep his impossible-seeming promises through sending his Son, Jesus, to be his promised King. This is good news of great joy!

In his baptism, Jesus showed he had come to be identified with sinners. In his temptation in the wilderness, Jesus showed he would perfectly obey his Father.

⊕ talkabout

1. When was the last time you were surprised by Jesus—by something he said or did, or a way he has worked in your life?

   • Did you feel uncomfortable, or threatened, or thrilled, or something else?

⊌ investigate

▸ Read Luke 4 v 14-30

2. What does Jesus claim about himself in verse 21?

DICTIONARY

Anointed (v 18): in Old Testament Israel, oil was poured over someone's head (an "anointing") to show they had been chosen for a particular role.
Elijah, Elisha (v 25,27): two Old Testament prophets. Both were rejected in Israel and performed miracles outside their homeland.

• What does Jesus' choice of passage tell us about his view of his mission (v 18-19—look also at v 43)?

Jesus is in the town "where he had been brought up" (v 16). And the townspeople are "amazed at the gracious words that came from his lips" (v 22).

3. But what seems to confuse them (v 22)?

4. What does Jesus realize is going on under the surface (v 23-27)?

• How does the townspeople's reaction prove his point (v 28-29)?

▶ Read Luke 4 v 31-44

The powerful works of Jesus that conclude this chapter serve almost as sermon illustrations for his sermon in verses 18-21.

DICTIONARY

Rebuked (v 39): told off sharply.
Proclaim (v 43): declare; share news.

5. How do we see Jesus beginning to fulfill Isaiah's prophecies about him in these acts?

⊡ apply

The people of Nazareth seem to have expected that they had a right to Jesus' blessings and miracles because they were from his hometown— because of who they were. But they found themselves watching Jesus' back as he walked away from them.

6. What sorts of people consider themselves to have a "right" to Jesus' blessings or help today? Why?

• How is Jesus' view of the people he has come to bless very different (v 18-19)? How does viewing ourselves in this "category" mean we treat Jesus very differently?

⊡ getting personal

Don't miss the opportunity to take stock of your presumptions; commit yourself to coming to Jesus on the basis of his kindness and mercy, and not on the basis of any merit of your own.

⏬ investigate

❯ Read Luke 5 v 1-28

In these verses, we see Jesus calling people into his kingdom, and doing all that is needed to bring them in. Luke is building up a picture of the sort of people who are in his kingdom, and the right response to his work of bringing people into the kingdom.

7. Complete the table to fill out the picture.

WHO DOES JESUS CALL OR HELP?	WHAT DOES HE DO FOR THEM, AND WHAT DOES IT REVEAL ABOUT HIM?	WHAT RIGHT RESPONSE TO HIM DO WE SEE?
v 2-3	v 4-7	v 8-11
v 12	v 13	n/a
v 18	v 20-21	v 26
v 27	n/a	v 28

▶ Read Luke 5 v 29-39

8. Where is all this taking place (v 29)?

9. The religious leaders, the Pharisees, have two issues with Jesus' conduct. What do their two comments (v 30, 33) reveal those two issues to be?

10. How does Jesus describe his mission in verses 31-32? How have we seen him enacting this mission in his words and actions from 4 v 14 to this point?

• Who are the self-proclaimed "healthy" people in this section of the Gospel?

⊡ **explore more**

optional

If the Pharisees' first accusation (v 30) was about who Jesus called into his kingdom, the second (v 33) is about the behavior of those who are part of his kingdom.

Fasting was a sign of mourning (whether for sin or over circumstances) and/or hopeful dissatisfaction with the present state of things (e.g. Anna, in 2 v 36-38).

So, as Jesus' short story in 5 v 34-35 shows, why does it not make sense for Jesus' followers to fast?

Jesus' arrival has changed everything.

How does his image in verses 36-38 reinforce this?
Can you think of times that your expectations of following Jesus and his demands about following him have been different? Were you tempted to stick with what you knew and understood, rather than letting him change everything?

⮕ apply

11. Why, if you think of yourself as spiritually "healthy," will you not only misunderstand Jesus, but be angered or upset by Jesus?

12. How does Peter (v 8-11) show us what it means to be someone who is spiritually ill, but who has been healed by Doctor Jesus?

⊡ getting personal

The eighteenth-century slave-trader-turned-pastor John Newton said on his deathbed, "My memory is nearly gone, but I remember two things: that I am a great sinner and that Christ is a great Savior."

Are these two things fundamental to your view of yourself and your salvation? How will that change your attitude to your failings and to your purpose this week?

⬆ pray

Use verses 8-11 to direct your prayers of confession and thanksgiving. Commit together to being willing to leave everything and follow Christ.

Luke 6 v 1 – 7 v 50
4 HOW TO BE HAPPY

The story so far

God worked to keep his impossible-seeming promises through sending his Son, Jesus, to be his promised King. This is good news of great joy!

In his baptism, Jesus showed he had come to be identified with sinners. In his temptation in the wilderness, Jesus showed he would perfectly obey his Father.

Jesus came as a doctor for the spiritually "sick," calling surprising people into his kingdom even as many "healthy" religious people rejected him.

⊕ **talkabout**

1. If you asked 10 people who live near you, "Where is real happiness to be found?," what kinds of answers do you think you would get?

• How would *you* answer that question?

⊍ **investigate**

❯ Read Luke 6 v 12-26 (6 v 1-26)

Two incidents deepen the conflict between Jesus and the religious leaders (v 1-5 and v 6-11), leaving "the Pharisees and the teachers of the law ... furious" and plotting against him (v 11). Against that backdrop,

Jesus chooses twelve of his disciples to become his inner circle. Then he begins to teach them about the life of those who follow him as King.

2. Fundamentally, these verses are about the distinction between two kinds of people. How does Jesus describe those types (v 20-23 and v 24-26)?

• Where does each group enjoy their "reward" (v 23-24)?

3. How is Jesus redefining what it means to be happy, or "blessed"?

⊡ **getting personal**

Jesus does not imagine a situation where a person can enjoy both the present pleasures of this world and also the joys of next world. We must choose our allegiance and the location of our ultimate joy.

What are you choosing? Where are you looking for your happiness? What about when it comes to your family? Does anything need to change?

▶ **Read Luke 6 v 27-49**

4. What does it mean for a follower of King Jesus to "love" (v 27-36)?

DICTIONARY

Hypocrite (v 42): someone who claims to be, or to believe, something, but whose actions disagree with that claim.

• When someone loves in this way, what are they demonstrating about their identity, and about whose example they are following (v 35b-36)?

5. What does Jesus warn us against in verses 41-42?

• Does this mean that a Christian should not judge that someone else is living wrongly, and point it out to them? Why/why not?

• How do verses 41-42 shape our understanding of what Jesus is (and is not) saying in verse 37?

6. How do you recognize what kind of tree you are looking at (v 43-45)? How about what kind of person?

• So where is Jesus saying that real change must always begin?

⊖ apply

7. Which aspect of Jesus' "Sermon on the Plain" do you find:

• most liberating?

• most counter-cultural?

• most personally challenging?

⊡ explore more

▶ Read Luke 7 v 1-17

In what unexpected place does Jesus find faith (v 1-10)?

How does Jesus show his power in verses 11-17?

Those who see the widow's son raised realize that, in Jesus, "God has come to help his people" (v 16).

How do these two episodes reveal who God's people are, and what help God has come to give them?

⊍ investigate

▶ Read Luke 7 v 18-50

8. Which two people are confused about whether Jesus really is the promised Messiah and a true prophet (v 18-19, 39)?

DICTIONARY

Dirge (v 32): a slow, sad song.
Denarii (v 41): a single denarius was worth about a laborer's daily wage.

John's confusion is understandable. He had promised that the one coming after him would "baptize you with the Holy Spirit and fire. His winnowing fork is in his hand to clear his threshing floor and to gather the wheat into his barn, but he will burn up the chaff with unquenchable fire" (3 v 16-17). But Jesus is seemingly on a do-good campaign of healing and preaching, showing mercy to Roman army officials (7 v 1-10)!

9. But what kind of Messiah is Jesus (v 21-22)?

• How are his actions and words toward the sinful woman in verses 48-50 consistent with his answer to John?

It turns out that the very miracles and welcomes that made John unsure about Jesus were actually the things that showed that Jesus was the Messiah. John was not wrong on the facts; there will be a time for judgment. But he was wrong about the timing; now is the time for healing and patience and forgiveness and good news.

10. Who grasps this, and who does not (v 29-30, 37-39)?

11. What is the correct answer to Jesus' question in verses 41-42? (Hint: You can use verse 43 to check your answer!)

- So what is the key to loving Jesus more (v 47)?

⮕ apply

12. How can we speak in ways that belittle or undermine our sinfulness? Why is that dangerous for Christians to do?

- What is the connection between knowing we have been forgiven greatly… loving Jesus increasingly… and living out his commands in the Sermon on the Plain?

⬆ pray

Thank Jesus for all you have seen of his character and standards in this study. Then use your answers to Question Seven as the basis for your requests to God. Finish by acknowledging your sinfulness, thanking Jesus for his forgiveness, and speaking to him of your love for him.

5

Luke 8 v 1-56
OF SOILS AND STORMS

The story so far

In his baptism, Jesus showed he had come to be identified with sinners. In his temptation in the wilderness, Jesus showed he would perfectly obey his Father.

Jesus came as a doctor for the spiritually "sick," calling surprising people into his kingdom even as many "healthy" religious people rejected him.

In his teaching and his treatment of others, Jesus showed that happiness lies in following him, loving like him, trusting him, and grasping forgiveness from him.

⊕ talkabout

1. Why do people fear things?

   • Is fear ever a good thing? Why/why not?

⊕ investigate

   ▶ Read Luke 8 v 1-21

   The first sentence of verse 18 is a good summary of the whole of Jesus' teaching in this passage.

2. What do we need to do? What different ways are there to "listen" to someone?

   DICTIONARY

   A hundred times more (v 8): that is, an amazingly huge crop.

3. What do the four types of soil in verses 5-8 represent (v 11-15)?

• How does this show us what listening well means?

Some hear the word with a good heart; these are the ones who have and who "will be given more" (v 18); they will bear fruit exponentially and receive many blessings from Christ. Those who hear the word with a bad heart ultimately find that they have lost it.

⊡ explore more

optional

What has been "given" to the disciples (v 10)?
What purpose do the parables have for those who have not been given this (v 10)?

These things are called "secrets," not because they are obscure and shadowy but because they can only be known if God chooses to reveal them. The quote from Isaiah is meant to have the effect of shocking the crowd into truly hearing. And the way to hear well is to ask for the ability to hear well—to understand and respond to Jesus' words (v 9).

How does this humble you as a Christian?
How might it affect the way you speak to those who are not Christians?

4. Who does Jesus define as being part of his family (v 19-21)?

• How does this motivate us to listen well?

☺ **getting personal**

Examine your life: do you exercise care in how you respond to the word of God? Can you point to places in your life where you have done something (or refrained from doing something) simply because you wanted to put Jesus' words into practice?

Are there ways that you have allowed the devil, or life's trials, or the deceitfulness of riches to choke out the growth of God's word?

⊖ **apply**

5. What would it look like to be a member of your church, while also being:
    • path-like ground?

    • rocky ground?

    • thorny ground?

    • Which type would you be most likely to become without even noticing?

⊥ investigate

❯ Read Luke 8 v 22-56

The second half of Luke 8 consists of three dramatic stories covering four of Jesus' miracles. Each story emphasizes Jesus' power and authority, and implicitly calls for a response in those who hear about it. The best way to understand them is to look at them together.

6. For each episode, sum up who Jesus helps, and how, in a sentence:

• v 22-25

• v 26-39

• v 40-56 (you can take two sentences for this one!)

7. How does each episode show us people (or a person) in a "storm," literal or otherwise?

8. What does each reveal about the nature of Jesus' power?

9. Who is (or appears to be) afraid, and why (v 24, 25, 28-29, 36-37, 47-48, 49-50)?

• Which fears does Jesus remove? Which does he not?

➔ apply

10. What do these three episodes teach us to do when we are afraid?

• Is fear ever a good thing? Why/why not?

11. How do these episodes teach us to encourage others when they are facing storms?

⊡ **getting personal**

It is easy to trust God when the sailing is smooth. But we can tell a great deal about what we really believe when we see how we respond in a time of crisis.

What do your responses to the storms of life suggest to you about your faith?

Feel that challenge, if you need to. And then remember the good news: that Jesus helps us—as he helped his disciples—even when we fail to trust him in the way that we should.

⬆ **pray**

Pray for:

• ears that listen.

• a life of obedience.

• a godly response to your fear.

Share any storms that you feel you are facing right now, or that those who are close to you face, and then bring your requests to your storm-stilling King.

6 Luke 9 v 1-62
FOLLOWING THE KING

The story so far

Jesus came as a doctor for the spiritually "sick," calling surprising people into his kingdom even as many "healthy" religious people rejected him.

In his teaching and his treatment of others, Jesus showed that happiness lies in following him, loving like him, trusting him, and grasping forgiveness from him.

Jesus' parables warn us to listen well by obeying him, as members of his family; his actions show that he has power over nature, evil, illness and even death.

⊕ talkabout

1. If you could have any job in the world, what would it be? Why?

⬇ investigate

❯ Read Luke 9 v 1-17

2. What job does Jesus invite his disciples to share with him (v 1-2)?

> **DICTIONARY**
>
> **Testimony (v 5):** a true message, or accurate verdict.

3. What job does he command his disciples to do in verse 13? What is the problem with the command?

• How does Jesus make it possible for his disciples to do this job (v 16-17)?

Between these two episodes, Luke tells us of King Herod's response to what is going on. Herod asks a question that is familiar to us by now: "Who … is this" (v 9)?

Even the ruler of the land lacks clarity. Luke is preparing us for the first human to grasp the truth about Jesus…

▶ Read Luke 9 v 18-20

4. What is Peter's answer to the question, "Who is this?" (v 20)?

• **Read 2 Samuel 7 v 12-13; Psalm 2; Jeremiah 23 v 5-6.** By answering Jesus' question as he does, what exactly is Peter saying about who Jesus is?

⤷ apply

5. What have these verses taught us about the work of Christian ministry?

• Why do Christians have a privileged job? To what extent do you view this job as a privilege?

⊡ getting personal

Jesus could have fed the crowd by himself. Instead, he involved the disciples in the work, and as a result they got the joy of service and a lesson about Jesus' power.

Is this how you view your own ministry—the ways you seek to serve others for Jesus and speak to others about Jesus?

What does your prayer life suggest about who you rely on when it comes to doing (or not doing) ministry?

⊻ investigate

❯ Read Luke 9 v 21-27

Remember the Old Testament background to the title of "Messiah."

6. What is shocking about verse 22?

DICTIONARY
Forfeit (v 25): give up.

7. What will life as a subject of the Messiah be like (v 23)? What do these phrases mean for everyday life?

• Why is it worth it (v 24-26)?

▶ **Read Luke 9 v 28-43a**

Take a moment to imagine the scene, as best you can.

8. Given what the disciples have heard in verses 21-26, why are verses 29 and 35 very significant?

DICTIONARY

Perverse (v 41): wrong, in a way that causes offense.

⊡ explore more

Literally, the word translated "departure" in verse 31 is "exodus."

With whom does Jesus talk about his "exodus" (v 30-31)?

❯ Read Exodus 12 v 21-32

When Israel were in slavery in Egypt under the power of the Egyptian Pharaoh, what plague did God send (v 29-30)?
How did Israel escape this judgment (v 21-23)?
What did this achieve (v 31-32)?

Moses, Elijah and Jesus think of the events Jesus will face in Jerusalem—his rejection, death and resurrection—as his "exodus."

How does this help us understand why God's plan was for his Messiah to die in this way?

Luke 9 v 37-43 is a powerful reminder that the Son of God did not come to live in glory here on earth, but to wade into human misery and set captives free (see 4 v 18).

❯ Read Luke 9 v 43b-62

We know that Jesus will be killed (v 22). And we know that this "departure" will take place in Jerusalem (v 31).

DICTIONARY
Samaritan (v 52): Jews hated people from the neighboring region of Samaria.

9. So how is verse 51 a turning point in the Gospel? What is Jesus now deliberately walking toward?

From this point on, we will see fewer miracles, fewer extended blocks of public teaching, and fewer crowds, as the narrative drives towards the climax of Jesus' crucifixion, resurrection and ascension into heaven.

10. What lessons about following Jesus do we get in this section?
   • v 46-48

- v 49-50

- v 52-56 (see 9 v 5)

- v 57-62

⊃ apply

11. In which parts of your lives do you find it hardest to hear Jesus' words in verse 22 and actually "listen to him"?

12. Why is following Jesus a wonderful "job"?

↑ pray

Use verses 20-22 to praise Jesus for who he is and why he came, reflecting on ways in which you are personally particularly grateful to him right now.

Then use verse 23 to prompt yourself to pray that you would follow him well. And ask for grace to be able to "listen to him."

7

Luke 10 v 1 – 11 v 36

YOU KNOW THE KINGDOM HAS COME

The story so far

In his teaching and his treatment of others, Jesus showed that happiness lies in following him, loving like him, trusting him, and grasping forgiveness from him.

Jesus' parables warn us to listen well by obeying him, as members of his family; his actions show that he has power over nature, evil, illness and even death.

Jesus is the all-powerful, glorious Messiah—but he came to be rejected and killed, and he calls people to pick up their own cross in order to follow him.

⊕ talkabout

1. What would you say are the main characteristics of your nationality, would you say?

• Do you feel proud of your nationality? What difference does that make to how you live?

⬇ investigate

> **Read Luke 10 v 1-24**

2. Jesus now appoints "seventy-two others" to go ahead of him. What does he tell them they should pray (v 2)?

DICTIONARY

Sodom (v 12): a city destroyed by God to punish its wickedness (Genesis 19).

Tyre and Sidon (v 13): Gentile cities north of Galilee, that Jesus never went to.

• What does he tell them they should expect (v 3)?

• What does he tell them they should proclaim (v 8-11)?

3. What warning does Jesus give the towns where he is sending these seventy-two followers (v 12-16)?

4. Why do the seventy-two return "with joy" (v 17)?

• Where does Jesus point them for their main source of joy (v 20-21)? Why does he do this, do you think?

☐ **getting personal**

Is your source of joy what you do for Jesus, or what you do for yourself, or what he has done for you?

⊡ explore more

> **Read Luke 10 v 25-37**

Jesus' famous story in verses 30-35 is told in response to two
questions that an "expert in the law" asks him.

What is the first, and how does Jesus answer it (v 25-28)?
Why is the expert in the law not satisfied with this (v 29)?
How does Jesus' parable define who a "neighbor" is?

After Jesus defined the man's obligation to neighbor-love in the
broadest terms, unasked questions linger in the air: *Do you still want
to depend on your obedience to the law? Are you still interested in
justifying yourself in order to gain eternal life?*

We usually read this parable assuming that we are to be the Good
Samaritan.

*What happens if we read it thinking of ourselves, spiritually-speaking,
as the man who is attacked?*

⊟ apply

Jesus' instructions in verses 1-24 are not meant as a step-by-step manual
for modern missions; these are instructions for a specific place and time.

5. But what does this passage teach us about mission in terms of:

• its urgency?

• its high stakes?

• what should bring us joy?

⬇ investigate

❯ Read Luke 10 v 38 – 11 v 13

6. What is the one thing that will never be taken away from someone (v 38-42)?

• Why do Jesus' disciples, as they begin to be included in the work Jesus has come to do, need to remember this?

7. Jesus teaches his disciples the things that God loves to hear them pray about (11 v 2-4). What are they?

• What does Jesus teach us about why prayer is wonderful (v 5-13)?

☺ getting personal

If you do not pray much, perhaps you have not appreciated the fact that God is your heavenly Father... or that God is willing to hear your prayers... or that God is able to give you all you need. Let Jesus' words here encourage you to pray; your Father is ready to hear you and bless you.

How will this affect your prayers this week?

▶ Read Luke 11 v 14-28 (11 v 14-36)

Jesus has told his followers to proclaim his kingdom
(10 v 9-11) and to pray for his kingdom to come
(11 v 2); and now he gets into an argument about
the nature of his kingdom.

DICTIONARY

Beelzebul (15):
another name for
Satan.

8. When Jesus drives out a demon, what accusation is made about the
nature of his kingdom (v 15)?

9. What answer does Jesus give (v 17-18)? How does this prove that he is
not working for Satan?

10. What *is* his work evidence of (v 20-22)?

11. What is the key application of Jesus' teaching here (v 28)?

• From the passages we've looked at in this study, what does it look like
to obey the word of God?

⊡ explore more

optional

The people had asked Jesus "for a sign from heaven" (v 16). In verse 29, he gets round to responding to the request.

What is the only "sign" they will be given (v 29-30)?

▶ Read Jonah 1 v 15-17; 2 v 10 – 3 v 10

The "sign" Jesus speaks of is likely someone going to a place of the dead (the belly of a fish, or the tomb) and coming back from there, alive, warning of judgment and offering salvation.

What was the right response to the "sign of Jonah" (Luke 11 v 32)? Why do the generation alive in Jesus' day therefore have no excuse for rejecting his message?

⊟ apply

12. How do verses 14-26 show us that, when it comes to Jesus, there is no middle ground?

• What implications are there for us in our view of the world, and our ambitions in this world?

⬆ pray

Use the prayer Jesus teaches his followers in verses 2-4 to shape your prayers together. And enjoy speaking to the God who listens to you because he is a Father to you.

Luke 11 v 37 – 12 v 34
8 FREED FROM WORRY

The story so far

In his teaching and his treatment of others, Jesus showed that happiness lies in following him, loving like him, trusting him, and grasping forgiveness from him.

Jesus' parables warn us to listen well by obeying him, as members of his family; his actions show that he has power over nature, evil, illness and even death.

Joy is found in knowing God has given us a place in heaven, and in spending time with and speaking to him—not in what we have done for God.

⊕ talkabout

1. What do unreligious people worry about most, do you think?

• What about religious people?

⊎ investigate

> **Read Luke 11 v 37 – 12 v 12**

2. What surprises the Pharisee that Jesus is eating with (11 v 38)?

DICTIONARY

A tenth (11 v 42): the Old Testament Law instructed God's people to give a tenth of their produce (Deuteronomy 14 v 28-29).
Unmarked graves (v 44): walking over a grave made someone ceremonially unclean (i.e. unacceptable to God).
Yeast (12 v 1): a type of fungus used in dough, that expands and spreads throughout the dough to make it rise.

Jesus' response might strike us as extreme. But he saw what seemed to be an innocuous religious practice as a symbol of everything that was wrong with the Pharisees. Their obsession with washings was an exercise in missing the point akin to merely washing "the outside of the cup and dish" (v 39). While there may be nothing wrong with the exterior of a bowl, cleaning it is a meaningless exercise if the inside is filthy.

3. What aspects of the religious approach of the Pharisees and the experts in the law does Jesus take issue with?

• v 42

• v 43

• v 44

• v 46

• v 47-51

• v 52

4. What one word does Jesus use to describe the problem with the Pharisees (12 v 1)? What does this word mean (the image in 11 v 39 helps)?

• How far will this approach get them, does 12 v 2-3 show?

🔅 explore more

optional

This religious hypocrisy among God's people—looking good, with hearts full of pride and empty of love—was not a new problem.

❯ Read Isaiah 29 v 13; Hosea 6 v 1-6

How does God describe his problem with his people's attitude through these two prophets?
What does God really want (Hosea 6 v 6)?
If these prophets were around today, how might they find similar attitudes in our churches?

🔅 getting personal

Whenever Christians are tempted to pretend to be more holy than they are... whenever we are unwilling to confess sin and ask for help... whenever we establish our own man-made rules as the standard for everyone's holiness... whenever we are comfortable with private sins so long as they do not come to light... in those situations the yeast of the Pharisees is present.

Is that yeast at work in you in any way?

How will you use Luke 12 v 2-3 to remind you of the uselessness of this way of approaching your relationship with God?

What will be different about how you treat others, speak with others, or speak to God?

▶ Read Luke 12 v 13-34

Next, a man comes to Jesus for help with a family dispute regarding an inheritance (v 13). Instead of resolving the conflict, Jesus tells a parable that addressed a far more weighty matter.

5. What one word does Jesus use to describe the problem with the man's attitude (v 15)?

• How does the parable he tells show how far this approach to life will get someone (v 16-21)?

⇨ apply

6. What was the great aim of the Pharisees? What was the great aim of the man who asked Jesus the question in verse 13?

• How do those aims in life look in your society (and perhaps in your church)?

• Why do they provoke worry in people?

⊍ **investigate**

7. What does Jesus tell his "friends" that they should worry about (v 5, 9-10)?

Verse 5 reminds us that there is a God who will give us the justice we deserve for our sins, when they are all exposed (v 2). Hell is real, and people are put there. If you were searching for something to be worried about, that would be a good candidate.

8. But who are the people who do not need to fear this (v 8)?

9. Why else do God's people not need to worry?
• v 11-12

• v 24-28

• v 29-31

• v 32

☺ **getting personal**

Jesus tenderly urges his "little flock" to "not be afraid" (v 32).

How does this encourage you in your worries today? What difference could it make to remember that you are a chosen, precious member of the King's flock?

10. What is the sign that we have grasped that God is our Father as well as our Judge (v 33-34)?

• How is this approach to life the opposite to the approach of the man in the parable in verses 16-20?

We see in Jesus' words a reminder of the way that Luke's Gospel began. Zechariah (1 v 12-15a), Mary (1 v 29-30) and the shepherds (2 v 9-10) all heard their angelic visitors speak a word of joy and comfort to them in their fear. It was sensible to be afraid in the presence of one of God's angels (1 v 19), but these messengers were sent with news of great joy.

Here in chapter 12, we hear an echo of that pattern; the good news of Jesus is that God is a frightening Judge, but he has shown us great love and care for us in Christ. When we trust him, he replaces our anxiety with peace and our fear with joy. The King has come to bring the joy of his kingdom and salvation. Do not be afraid!

⊡ apply

11. How does the gospel expose and undermine the need for:
    • hypocrisy?

    • greed?

12. Reflect on Luke 1 – 12. How has looking at the coming of God's King, and his kingdom:
    • excited you?
    • surprised you?
    • challenged you?
    • liberated you from fear?

⊡ pray

Thank God for his shepherding, fatherly care for you. Pray for spiritual sight to see ways in which you might be guilty of religious hypocrisy or worldly greed. Then "cast all your anxiety on him because he cares for you" (1 Peter 5 v 7).

Leader's Guide: Luke 1 – 12

INTRODUCTION

Leading a Bible study can be a bit like herding cats—everyone has a different idea of what the passage could be about, and a different line of enquiry that they want to pursue. But a good group leader is more than someone who just referees this kind of discussion. You will want to:

* correctly understand and handle the Bible passage. But also…

* encourage and train the people in your group to do this for themselves. Don't fall into the trap of spoon-feeding people by simply passing on the information in the Leader's Guide. Then…

* make sure that no Bible study is finished without everyone knowing how the passage is relevant for them. What changes do you all need to make in the light of the things you have been learning? And finally…

* encourage the group to turn all that has been learned and discussed into prayer.

Your Bible-study group is unique, and you are likely to know better than anyone the capabilities, backgrounds and circumstances of the people you are leading. That's why we've designed these guides with a number of optional features. If they're a quiet bunch, you might want to spend longer on *talkabout*. If your time is limited, you can choose to skip *explore more*, or get people to look at these questions at home. Can't get enough of Bible study? Well, some studies have optional extra homework projects. As leader, you can adapt and select the material to the needs of your particular group.

So what's in the Leader's Guide?
The main thing that this Leader's Guide will help you to do is to understand the major teaching points in the passage you are studying, and how to apply them. As well as guidance for the questions, the Leader's Guide for each session contains the following important sections:

THE BIG IDEA

One or two key sentences will give you the main point of the session. This is what you should be aiming to have fixed in people's minds as they leave the Bible study. And it's the point you need to head back towards when the discussion goes off at a tangent.

SUMMARY

An overview of the passage, including plenty of useful historical background information.

OPTIONAL EXTRA

Usually this is an introductory activity that ties in with the main theme of the Bible study, and is designed to "break the ice" at the beginning of a session. Or it may be a "homework project" that people can tackle during the week.

So let's take a look at the various different features of a Good Book Guide:

⊕ talkabout

Each session kicks off with a discussion question, based on the group's opinions or experiences. It's designed to get people talking and thinking in a general way about the main subject of the Bible study.

⊕ investigate

The first thing you and your group need to know is what the Bible passage is about, which is the purpose of these questions. But watch out—people may come up with answers based on their experiences or teaching they have heard in the past, without referring to the passage at all. It's amazing how often we can get through a Bible study without actually looking at the Bible! If you're stuck for an answer, the Leader's Guide contains guidance for questions. These are the answers to direct your group to. This information isn't meant to be read out to people—ideally, you want them to discover these answers from the Bible for themselves. Sometimes there are optional follow-up questions (see ☑ in guidance for questions) to help you help your group get to the answer.

⊡ explore more

These questions generally point people to other relevant parts of the Bible. They are useful for helping your group to see how the passage fits into the "big picture" of the whole Bible. These sections are OPTIONAL—only use them if you have time. Remember that it's better to finish in good time having really grasped one big thing from the passage, than to try and cram everything in.

⊟ apply

We want to encourage you to spend more time working at application—too often, it is simply tacked on at the end. In the Good Book Guides, apply sections are mixed in with the investigate sections of the study. We hope that people will realize that application is not just an optional extra, but rather, the whole purpose of studying the

Bible. We do Bible study so that our lives can be changed by what we hear from God's word. If you skip the application, the Bible study hasn't achieved its purpose.

These questions draw out practical lessons that we can all learn from the Bible passage. You can review what has been learned so far, and think about practical differences that this should make in our churches and our lives. The group gets the opportunity to talk about what they personally have learned.

⊡ getting personal

These can be done at home, but it is well worth allowing a few moments of quiet reflection during the study for each person to think and pray about specific changes they need to make in their own lives. Why not have a time for reporting back at the beginning of the following session, so that everyone can be encouraged and challenged by one another to make application a priority?

⬆ pray

In Acts 4 v 25-30 the first Christians quoted Psalm 2 as they prayed in response to the persecution of the apostles by the Jewish religious leaders. Today however, it's not as common for Christians to base prayers on the truths of God's word as it once was. As a result, our prayers tend to be weak, superficial and self-centred rather than bold, visionary and God-centered.

The prayer section is based on what has been learned from the Bible passage. How different our prayer times would be if we were genuinely responding to what God has said to us through his word.

1

Luke 1 v 1 – 2 v 40
NOTHING IS IMPOSSIBLE

THE BIG IDEA
God keeps his impossible promises—we are to respond to his work to bring his King to this world with trust and joy.

SUMMARY
The first two chapters of Luke, often referred to as the "Infancy Narrative," are particularly memorable for their angelic visitations and vivid accounts of otherwise insignificant people who are swept up in God's great plan of redemption. The story begins in the days of Herod, who reigned in Israel under Roman authority from 37 BC – 4 BC.

Through the angel's visits to Zechariah (1 v 5-25) and Mary (v 26-38), God intervenes directly after hundreds of years without a prophet in Israel. Both pregnancies are miraculous (Elizabeth is barren; Mary is a virgin); both children are part of the fulfillment of God's promises: John is to be a prophet, announcing the arrival of Jesus, God's promised King, who will save his people. Those who grasp what God is doing respond with joy—today, as then. This study focuses on the trustworthiness of God's promises, impossible though they may seem—and the joy of living by faith in King Jesus.

OPTIONAL EXTRA
Come up with a list of promises (such as "I promised to bake you a cake," "I promise to fill out your tax return accurately," "I promise to build your home an extension" and ask each member of your group to say who else in the group they would most like, and least like(!) to hear each promise from. The point is to see that the identity of a promise-maker is in many ways more important than the nature of the promise itself and can cause joy, or terror!

GUIDANCE FOR QUESTIONS
1. Whose promises do you most trust, and why? Whose promises do you least trust, and why? This question introduces the idea that the character and ability of someone who is making a promise are as important as the content of that promise. You may not believe someone who promises to meet you at 4pm the next day because you know they are unreliable. Equally, you may believe someone else's promise to love you faithfully for the rest of your life, because you know they are trustworthy. The promise is bigger and harder to keep, but the character and ability of the person are such that you can trust them.

You could return to this idea after Q3, 5 or 12, and think about how God's character and ability are such that we are able to trust in his promises, even though they are big and hard to keep—impossible for humans, in fact. In one sense, Luke 1 v 1-56 are about God's impossible promises, to individuals and to his people as a whole, and 1 v 57 – 2 v 40 are about God working to keep those promises.

2. Why is Luke writing (v 4)? To give Theophilus, and all his readers, "certainty" (v 4) about what they have heard/been taught about Jesus. **How do v 1-3 give us confidence in what he is writing?** This guide to the life of Jesus is based on information from reputable sources who were really in a position to know the truth—

"eyewitnesses and servants of the word" (v 2). Luke has carefully followed these things for quite some time, and he has been on a mission to compile an "orderly account" (v 3) of all "the things that have been fulfilled among us" (v 1). Luke expresses no interest in passing on rumors or hearsay. He is preserving an accurate record of what really happened. So we can trust it!

3. Why are both [Elizabeth's and Mary's pregnancies] impossible?

- Mary is a virgin (v 27, 34). Virgins cannot, by definition, be pregnant!
- Elizabeth is "very old" and was "unable to conceive" (v 36—see v 7). Very old women cannot have children (and Elizabeth had always been unable to fall pregnant).

- **Why does Mary know they will happen (v 37-38)?** Gabriel tells Mary that "no word from God will ever fail" (v 37). She does not need to know the mechanics of how it will happen; she only need be confident that the Lord has declared that it will happen. His word never fails (some Bibles translate v 37 as "nothing is impossible with God"). Mary knows that God will fulfill his "word to me" (v 38) and is willing to be humbly obedient to it.

4. What is God like, according to Mary's "song" in verses 46-55?

- He is a personal Savior (v 47).
- He cares about individuals, however lowly they may be in worldly terms (v 48).
- He is mighty and holy (v 49).
- He is merciful to those who "fear" (i.e. live in awe of) him (v 50).
- In his might, he humbles those who are successful and proud, and lifts up those who are humble and know their need (v 51-53).
- He keeps his promises to his people (Old Testament Israel) (v 54-55). Mary sees the

birth of her son as an expression of God's faithfulness to keep his ancient promises to Abraham and his descendants.

- **Mary's son is "the Son of the Most High," whose "kingdom will never end" (v 32-33). What does her song leave us expecting her child to do?** He will be a King who is all the things Mary sings about. In one sense, Mary sings not only "up" to God, but "down" to God growing as a baby in her womb. Her son is God's Son, the eternal King, who will fulfill all God's promises throughout the Old Testament. Mary's song gives us a flavor of what her child will be like and what he will do.

5. Track Mary's responses to what is going on in v 29-30, 38, 46-47.

- Initially, Mary is afraid—"greatly troubled" (v 29-30). God becoming involved in life is rarely comfortable; it is unsettling.
- She submits to his plan (v 38)—she is humble, seeing herself as "the Lord's servant." She believes that God will do what he has said.
- She "glorifies the Lord" (literally "magnifies the Lord"), and she rejoices over who God is and what he is doing in her life" (v 46-47). Usually when we speak of magnifying something, we are making something larger than it really it is. When Mary magnifies the Lord, she isn't making him bigger; she's increasing the love and joy and worship of her heart until it is more in line with how great God is .

What does she show us about what true faith looks like? True faith does not mean never being unsettled or troubled by what God is doing or calling us to. But it does mean submitting humbly to his plans, believing his promises and seeking to bring our view of him into line with how great he really is. And true faith affects our emotions—it causes us to rejoice about who God is and how he has fulfilled his promises in Mary's baby.

6. APPLY: Why, and when, do we find it hard to live with Mary-like faith? Give your group time to think about areas of their lives, or circumstances of their lives, where they find it difficult to:

• submit to God's plan (especially when it may be costly to them and their own plans).
• believe in God's promises because they seem impossible.
• rejoice, allowing their affections to be shaped by their relationship with the mighty God.

Aim to move your group on to thinking about how they might encourage themselves (or each other) to have a Mary-like faith in their own spiritual lives.

EXPLORE MORE
Why did Mary and Joseph travel to Bethlehem (2 v 1-5)? Because Augustus, the Roman emperor, instructed everyone throughout the Roman empire to travel to their ancestral home in order to register (v 3). Augustus was the most powerful man in the known world, flattered by the Roman governing senate as the "son of a god." **[Read 2 Samuel 7 v 11b-16 and Micah 5 v 2-4.] Why is Bethlehem significant? Who would be born there?** God had promised David, the shepherd who he had made king over his people, that he would have a greater descendant who would rule his people for ever. And he had promised through Micah that this King, the one who would shepherd God's people, would be born in Bethlehem.

How does this show that Augustus is not quite as powerful as it appeared, and that his empire is not quite as

important as it seemed? Augustus' order to gather for a census was under the control of God. God was the prime mover, not the emperor. And the baby born in the most humble beginnings truly was the Son of the Most High. He would reign on David's throne, in an eternal kingdom that puts Augustus' rule to shame (Luke 1 v 32-33).

7. On the night that Mary has her baby (2 v 6-7), what does an angel tell some shepherds nearby about who that baby is (v 10-12)?
A Savior—a rescuer
The Messiah—God's promised, forever-ruling King
The Lord—a term reserved by Jews for God himself
Notice that his arrival is "good news that will cause great joy" (v 10).

8. What responses to God's work that night do we see here?

• v 9: Terror. God's glory—his presence—is terrifying, because he is holy and we are not (see Isaiah 6 v 1-5). It is in this context that the angel encourages them not to be afraid—God has not come to judge, but to save (Luke 2 v 10)
• v 14: Praise. The angels model the right response to the events of this night as they glorify God.
• v 18: Amazement. If we do not find the first Christmas amazing, we haven't understood it!
• v 19: Treasuring up and pondering what is happening. Unsurprisingly, Mary took time (a whole lifetime, we could say) to process what God had done through her and around her!
• v 20: Glorifying and praising God. The shepherds, having seen for themselves the truth of the angel's message, copy the company of angels.

9. What have Simeon and Anna been waiting for (v 25-26, 36-38)?

- "The consolation of Israel" (v 25), a phrase that conjures up Isaiah's prophecies about the arrival of the Lord's comfort and compassion (Isaiah 40 v 1-2; 49 v 13).
- Seeing "the Lord's Messiah" (Luke 2 v 26): God's Spirit had communicated to Simeon that he would see the long-awaited King before he died.
- "The redemption of Jerusalem" (v 38), a phrase referring to the freeing of God's people from their enemies (Isaiah 52 v 9).
- **Both realize that, in the baby Jesus, they are looking at the end of their time of waiting. What does this tell us about what this baby has been born to do?** Again, Luke is showing us that the infant Jesus is the fulfillment of God's promises to his people. Simeon and Anna remind us that the faithful people of Israel were engaged in a long process of waiting for God's act of salvation to come. Now, with this baby, that act has arrived, and the waiting is over. God's promises, which must have sometimes seemed so impossible, are going to be fulfilled in him. Simeon is able to say to God that "my eyes have seen your salvation" (Luke 2 v 30) as he looks at the child in his arms.

10. What does Simeon tell Mary in verses 34-35?

- Her child is destined to be the cause of the falling and rising of many in Israel.
- Her child will be "spoken against."
- His life will reveal what people really think.
- "A sword will pierce your own soul too."
- **How is this a jarring note amid all the joy surrounding Jesus' birth?** Because it suggests division, rejection and deep pain. Simeon is prophesying about Jesus' ministry, which will effectively split the

nation of Israel in two as many see him as someone who must be spoken against, even as many others (including Gentiles—non-Jews—v 32) see him as their Savior. **What do you think it is talking about?** This enigmatic comment about a sword piercing Mary's soul is the first time amid all the joy of his birth that Jesus' cross looms in the distance. This child will indeed redeem Israel, and will be the bringer of great joy—but it will be through pain and at cost that he does so.

11. Imagine you had never heard of Jesus or read the Bible, and you had picked up Luke's Gospel and reached 2 v 40. What would you think about:
- **who this baby is?**
- **what he has come to do?**

This question recaps your answers to Q4, 7 and 9-10. Don't underestimate the massive nature of the claims that are being made about this baby—about his identity and about his work. The question we should ask through the rest of the Gospel is, Can this man deliver on these claims?

12. APPLY: What reactions of people who truly realize who Jesus is has Luke shown us? Joyful praise; humble awe; sharing the news with others. At the heart of real faith in the gospel is the joy of realizing that in his great love God has sent his salvation to people by fulfilling all his promises in his Son. No wonder Christians have spent the last 2,000 years joining the shepherds in "glorifying and praising God for all the things they [have] heard and seen" (v 20)! **How would these look in our lives today?** Again, a chance for your group to be practical and specific

.

2

Luke 2 v 41 – 4 v 13
STANDING IN OUR SHOES

THE BIG IDEA
Jesus came to identify with us so that we could be identified with him, enjoying the verdict and status with God the Father that his obedience deserves.

SUMMARY
This study focuses on two scenes. The first is Jesus' baptism by John (3 v 21-22), where he identifies with sinful people, so that sinful people might be able to be identified with him—with the Son of God, who always pleases his loving Father. The second is Jesus' temptation by Satan, where Jesus, empowered by the Spirit, resists the devil's lures, proving himself to be the Son of God, who will succeed where both Adam and Israel failed (see Explore More). And, since as sinners Jesus is our only hope, his victory over Satan here (and supremely at the cross) is precious, because his victory is our victory too. Jesus defies Satan in the desert not primarily as our example but as our Savior.

OPTIONAL EXTRA
Split your group into two, and assign one on each team to play a game against one another (e.g. a best-of-five contests of Rock-Paper-Scissors). The winner will win a prize for their whole team. Inevitably, each "team" will support the member who is actually playing, without you needing to tell them to. Afterwards, ask them why—it will be because the person playing was "their guy," and because their prize rested on their guy's performance. So it is with Jesus—he is the One who represents us, and wins salvation for us through his performance. Return to this idea after Q5, 6 and/or 10.

GUIDANCE FOR QUESTIONS
1. Why do people get so joyful and/ or so sad about the fortunes of the sporting teams they support? The aim of this question is to introduce the idea of identifying with someone else, or seeing someone else (or some team) as your representatives. They carry your hopes, and their successes and failures are yours because you identify with them. A sporting fan does not contribute to his team's victory but he links his joys and sadnesses to that victory, or defeat. Sports fans are loyal to their team because they identify with them. In this study, we will be discovering how Jesus identifies with humanity so that humans might be identified with him. He therefore represents his people—his victories or defeats will be theirs. So you could link this question to our identity with and in Christ after Q3, in answering Q6, and/or during Q10 and 11.

2. What was baptism by John, Jesus' relative, "for" (that is, a sign of—3 v 3)? Repentance for the forgiveness of sins. Repentance involves choosing to turn the course of one's life; it involves both turning away from a fundamental commitment to sin and turning toward the Lord in obedience. To be baptized by John was to make a public declaration of repentance and an acknowledgement of the need for forgiveness.

3. So when Jesus comes to be baptized (v 21), what kind of people is he identifying with? People who need to be forgiven for their sins—that is, sinners. Part of the glory of Jesus' incarnation is that God would willingly stoop into human history, sinful and broken as it is. His baptism is a powerful picture of that truth, that the sinless Son of God would be willing to identify himself with sinful humanity.

4. What is different, and unique, about Jesus' baptism (v 21-22)? Heaven opened and the Holy Spirit descended on Jesus, in the physical form of a dove. And then a voice from heaven (that is, God the Father's voice) is heard giving his verdict on Jesus: Jesus is his beloved Son, and he is "well pleased" with him (v 22). In a sinful world, here is a unique human—one about whose every thought, action and word God the Father says, *I am well pleased with you.*

5. Reading the Father's verdict on Jesus in verse 22, why is this [i.e. sinners being able to be identified with Jesus] brilliant news for us? Because Jesus went under the waters of baptism as a way of saying, *Consider me to be one of them, and consider them to be just like me.* Jesus willingly identified with sinful humanity, and bore humanity's punishment on the cross, so that sinful humans could be identified with his righteousness, his perfection (see 2 Corinthians 5 v 21). So now we enjoy the verdict Jesus deserves, if by faith we identify with him. His verdict is ours—God the Father calls us his children and chooses to look at us as though we are as righteous as Jesus is. Because God is pleased with Jesus, and because Jesus identifies with us, God is pleased with us.

6. APPLY: What difference does sharing in Jesus' standing before God make when:
• **we worry about what others think of us?** In Jesus, we are the righteousness

of God and so God (whose opinion truly matters in the end) approves of us 100%. We are loved by our Creator—he thinks as highly of us as he does his Son. Why be concerned about the opinions of others when we already enjoy his good opinion?

• **we become aware of our failings?** We do not need to be defensive or self-protective; neither should we resort to despair or self-loathing. Despite our sin, in Jesus we have perfect righteousness and are children of God. We do not need to be good to be saved. Our failings do not negate God's love for us because our goodness was never the grounds of his love for us. So we take our failings seriously, but we are not crushed by them.

• **we fulfill a great dream or achieve a success?** We don't think too highly of ourselves. None of our successes save us. Christ does, and has. We can enjoy success without craving it or relying on it.

7. Who is doing battle in the wilderness (4 v 1-2)? On the one hand there is "Jesus, full of the Holy Spirit." The Spirit "led" Jesus to this temptation. The Spirit's ministry was one of empowering and guiding Jesus. On the other side, we have the devil, tempting Jesus. Notice that we are not introduced to the devil or told anything about him; Luke seems to assume that his readers will be familiar with him. But as we read of the devil tempting the Son of God personally and verbally, Luke likely wants us to be thinking of the temptation of Adam and Eve in the Garden of Eden (see Genesis 3 v 1-6, where the devil appears in the form of a serpent and suggests that the first humans distrust the word of God).

EXPLORE MORE
Read Luke 3 v 23-38. Who else [besides

Jesus] is described as "the son of God" (v 38)? Adam. Both Adam and Jesus have no human, biological father; they own their descent directly to God himself.

Adam, the son of God and the image of God (Genesis 1 v 26-28), was created to represent God to the world. Read Genesis 3 v 1-19. What did he do instead, and with what results? He rejected his status of being a "son of God" and rebelled against his Creator. His relationship with God was fractured, and so was the image of God in him. And his relationships with his wife and with the rest of the creation were also broken.

Read Numbers 13 v 1-3; 13 v 26 – 14 v 4, 26-35. When they [Israel] were in the wilderness, how did the "son" treat his Father? God had promised Israel that he would give them victory over the wicked inhabitants of Canaan. But the people refused to trust his promise or believe he would come through for them; they rebelled against him and effectively called him an uncaring liar (14 v 3). They preferred slavery in Egypt to life under God's rule.

8. Think about what kind of life Satan is offering Jesus with each temptation.

1. The voice from heaven had declared that Jesus was God's Son (Luke 3 v 22); in 4 v 3 the devil seems to be asking why God's Son would have to experience this kind of hunger. After all, he possessed the power to make stones into bread if he wanted to (see 3 v 8). What the devil seems to be getting at, though, is not so much about food as it is about trust. Jesus has come in the flesh to identify with humanity so that he can save us. Now the immortal Son of God has taken on flesh with all of its limitations; he now feels exhaustion and hunger and thirst. And so what Satan is tempting him to is

something of a way out.

2. In 4 v 5-7, the devil is offering to Jesus a crown without a cross. The devil will share whatever limited authority and power that God has granted to him, and Jesus can have it without having to suffer. Jesus is being offered the chance to take a kind of glory and authority for himself, but without obeying his Father and saving his people.

3. In verses 9-11, the devil is offering to Jesus repute and respect from those around him. If the people see him jump from the top of the temple and God's angels catch him, it will prove beyond a shadow of a doubt who he is, and will see him embraced and hailed as the Messiah.

• **Why would each offer have been extremely tempting?** A way to escape the limitations of being a frail human… power and success without suffering… respect and status. We can all, in our own way, understand how tempting it is to disobey God in order to enjoy each of these. We are tempted in these ways, too.

9. Each time, Jesus stands firm and obeys his Father. What does the devil do next (v 13)? He leaves him till "an opportune time." The first round of the fight goes decisively to Jesus, and the devil retreats with his tail metaphorically tucked between his legs. But he will be back…

10. APPLY: How does that [our identification with Jesus, by faith] make his obedience in the wilderness precious for us? He stood in the desert and was tempted in our place. Where the other sons of God would not trust the word of the Lord but gave in to diabolic temptation, Jesus was faithful. By virtue of his faithful life and sacrificial death, his people are free from both the power and the penalty of sin (see Romans 6 v 5-14).

To put it another way, if Jesus had given in to the devil's second temptation, he would not have gone to the cross. Our entire salvation hangs on the content of his answer in Luke 4 v 8.

11. APPLY: What does the experience of Jesus in the wilderness teach us:

- **most importantly, about how we can respond when we give into temptation?** Our salvation does not hang on our obedience. When we sin, Satan will tempt us to despair and tell us that we cannot be forgiven, or that our sin does not matter so that we do not need to be forgiven. But our salvation hangs on Jesus' obedience, not on ours. Our sin does matter; but our sin is forgiven. Our obedience does matter; but it is Jesus' obedience that gives us eternal life, and he was obedient when he was tempted.

- **about how we go about resisting temptation?** Too often the story of the temptation of Jesus is reduced to a quarry from which we can mine strategies for resisting temptations ourselves. For example: Jesus quoted the Bible when he was tempted; so should we! So we should (and if your group come up with these kinds of answers, they are not wrong!) But there is actually much more going on here than that approach admits and that we easily miss. Jesus did not stand in the desert primarily as our example; he was there as our Savior. His victory in the desert becomes ours, and so we are no longer slaves to sin, unable to resist temptation. We fight against the allure of sin by going to Jesus in faith and prayer, knowing that the one who fought the tempter on our behalf is with us to help us in our time of need. We fight sin not in our strength, but in his.

Luke 4 v 14 – 5 v 32
3 INTO THE KINGDOM

THE BIG IDEA

Jesus called surprising people into his kingdom—and some surprising people ended up outside his kingdom. He is the doctor, who has come to help those who know they are spiritually sick, and those who see themselves as healthy will not like him.

SUMMARY

In this section of Luke's Gospel, we see very clearly that Jesus was not going to be the King that most people expected, and that some people continued to demand.

Having announced his identity as the Spirit-anointed deliverer, Jesus is rejected by his townspeople in Nazareth (4 v 14-30), seemingly because they consider themselves entitled to question him and deserving of his power and blessings. And his actions brings him into conflict with the religious leaders, who do not approve of his claims to be able to forgive sins (5 v 21) or of his calling sinful people to follow him (5 v 30). Yet alongside these rejections, Jesus calls people into his kingdom, and does everything necessary to enable them to come into that kingdom. As we see a sinful fisherman, a leper, a paralytic and a tax collector joyfully beginning new lives as part of his kingdom, we see the nature of the kingdom, and the response that the King calls for.

Jesus himself sums up what he is doing in 5 v 31-32—he is a doctor, who has come to help those who know they are sick. Those who think they are fine without him will never ask for help, and will miss out on his kingdom.

OPTIONAL EXTRA

In 5 v 31-32, Jesus talks about his mission in terms of a doctor to the sick. To introduce the idea of needing (if you are sick) to match up symptoms to a disease/medical issue, and then to a course of treatment, look up on a medical website the names, symptoms and treatments for a variety of illnesses. Then print them out on separate pieces of paper, so that your group (as a whole group, or in pairs or on their own) can match up the name of each illness with its symptoms, and its treatment. To recap Jesus' teaching visually, you could return to this activity at the end of the study, with "Sin-sick," "Envy, adultery, selfishness, immorality, malice [etc]," and "Jesus" written on separate pieces of paper—which describes our condition, its symptoms, and where we must turn for treatment.

GUIDANCE FOR QUESTIONS

1. When was the last time you were surprised by Jesus—by something he said or did, or a way he has worked in your life? In this section of Luke's Gospel, Jesus will surprise those who think they understand religion. We should expect him to surprise us still today. Your group may share how Jesus has led them in unexpected ways; or recall times when Jesus' ethical standards have been different, and more

difficult, than their own or those of their cultures; and so on.

- **Did you feel uncomfortable, or threatened, or thrilled, or something else?** Obviously, how someone feels about Jesus surprising them depends on the surprise. But point out (if you need to) that discovering that Jesus is different in some way than we had understood or assumed can be unsettling and threatening, because it poses us the challenge: will we mold ourselves to fit the reality of who he is and what he does, or we seek to mold him to fit in with our preferences?

2. What does Jesus claim about himself in 4 v 21? That the promises God had made through Isaiah seven centuries before were being fulfilled that very day, in the presence of the people listening. Jesus is telling them that he is the prophet (v 24) and the Messiah (the "anointed" one, v 18).

- **What does Jesus' choice of passage tell us about his view of his mission (v 18-19—look also at v 43)?** It seems that Jesus intentionally unrolled the scroll to a specific place in the text of Isaiah; notice that Luke tells us that Jesus "found the place where it is written" (v 17). In essence, Jesus sees himself as coming for "outsiders"—the poor, the oppressed, the imprisoned and the crippled—as the Spirit-anointed messenger of God's grace. Those who seem to have been beyond the reach of the "Lord's favor" are now recipients of his salvation. Of course, this is no surprise to Luke's readers; we have already been prepared for this reversal of fortune by Mary's reflection on this very theme in her song of praise (1 v 46-55, especially v 50-53).

Jesus' mission is therefore to "proclaim the good news of the kingdom of God" (v 43)—in Isaiah's terms, to "proclaim the year of the Lord's favor" (v 19). This is what he has been "sent" to do.

3. But what seems to confuse them [the townspeople] (v 22)? The issue of his origin. How has "Joseph's son" become such a powerful rabbi? Indeed, how can it be that "Joseph's son" is the Spirit-anointed fulfiller of all God's promises to his people?

4. What does Jesus realize is going on under the surface (v 23-27)? Jesus sees below the surface a fundamental rejection of his mission and ministry. He came to bring unmerited "good news to the poor" and "sight for the blind" (v 18), but they expected that they had a right to his blessings because they were from his hometown. They recognize that he has power and they marvel at his teaching, but they do not believe in him or his God-given mission. If the people have a proverb for Jesus (v 23), he has one for them as well: "no prophet is accepted in his hometown" (v 24).

Jesus' mention of incidents from the ministries of Elijah and Elisha (1 Kings 17 v 7-24 and 2 Kings 5 v 1-19a, respectively) serves a dual purpose. On one hand, it brings to mind the fact that these two prophets were rejected and persecuted during the course of their ministries. They were "Exhibit A and B" proving Jesus' point about prophets who were not accepted at home. On the other hand, both men had performed miracles outside of their homeland. Both Elijah and Elisha pointed forward to Jesus by reminding Israel that God shows his favor and mercy to unlikely people, in this case even Gentiles.

- **How does the townspeople's reaction prove his point (v 28-29)?** Their reaction is to reject him! They are furious (v 28) and seek to "throw him off the cliff" (v 29). In the end, all there is for Jesus to do is to escape the crowd's clutches (v 30), by what means we are not told.

5. How do we see Jesus beginning to fulfill Isaiah's prophecies about him in these acts [in 4 v 31-44]? In Capernaum, the anointing of the Spirit was demonstrated in the authority of his teaching (v 31-32), his ministry of healing the sick (v 38-40), and his power over impure spirits (v 33-35, 41). Both the people (v 36-37) and the demons (v 34, 41) are forced to acknowledge Jesus' power and authority to carry out his mission of good news. All these serve to validate Jesus' message—his mission to "proclaim the good news of the kingdom of God" (v 43).

6. APPLY: What sorts of people consider themselves to have a "right" to Jesus' blessings or help today? Why? Some possible answers:

- Religious people often think Jesus "owes" them blessing.
- Those brought up in Christian households, or "Christian countries," can assume Jesus will help and save them, whatever their own faith.
- Bible-study group members!

All these people (and many others) see Jesus' blessings as something to be earned by their merits—be it where or to whom they were born, or what they do.

- **How is Jesus' view of the people he has come to bless very different (v 18-19)?** Jesus' message is radical; he has been sent to the unlikely: the poor, the unimportant, and the outsider. **How does viewing ourselves in this "category" mean we treat Jesus very differently?** If we acknowledge that we bring nothing to the table when it comes to our relationship with Jesus and our enjoyment of his blessings, then we will be humble, grateful, and joyful (rather than having an attitude that is proud, entitled and ungrateful). We need to learn to read verses 18-19 as describing each of us. Spiritually speaking, we were in poverty, imprisoned by sin, and blind to the gospel.

7. Complete the table to fill out the picture [of Jesus bringing people into his kingdom]. See table below.

Who does Jesus call or help?
v 2-3: Simon, a fisherman
v 12: A leper (see note below this table)
v 18: a paralyzed man
v 27: Levi, a tax collector (see note below this table)

What does he do for them, and what does it reveal about him?
v 4-7: He gives them a miraculous catch of fish, so great that the boats almost sink. Jesus has control of nature.
v 13: He heals the man by his touch and his word. Jesus has power over disease (and he is willing to use it to break down barriers to his kingdom)
v 20-21: He forgives his sins. Jesus has the authority to forgive sins against God (v 24)

What right response to him do we see?
v 8: Peter asks Jesus to "go away"— because he has become aware of Jesus' divine holiness and his own sinfulness
v 10-11: Called to follow Jesus despite his sinfulness, he leaves everything he has ever known to follow him.

n/a
v 26: To be filled with awe and spontaneously be moved to praise God
v 28: Levi does the same thing Simon (and James and John) had done—he leaves everything to follow Jesus.

Note: Leprosy was so serious because the individual was considered ritually unclean and was required to live in isolation from the life of the community (see Leviticus 13 v 45-46). Merely entering a house where leprosy had broken out was enough to render an Israelite unclean (14 v 46, 54-57), and lepers were required to walk about announcing their wretched condition lest anyone accidentally come into contact with them and risk contracting their uncleanness.

Note: Tax collectors were normally Jews who were working for the Roman government, exacting the very taxes from their fellow-countrymen that served to support the forces that occupied their land. They were infamous for their treachery and willingness to collect more than they had a right to (see John the Baptist's admonition in Luke 3 v 12-13). Tax collectors were commonly viewed as the ultimate sinners, the enemies of God and his people.

8. Where is all this taking place (5 v 29)?
"A great banquet" held in Jesus' honor by Levi, attended by "a large crowd of tax collectors and others."

9. The religious leaders, the Pharisees, have two issues with Jesus' conduct. What do their two comments (v 30, 33) reveal those two issues to be?
• v 30: An issue with his choice of followers. What rabbi would allow such a person as Levi to be part of his inner circle, let alone command him to come after him?

- v 33: An issue with his followers' conduct. They point to the difference in practice between Jesus' followers and those of both John the Baptist and the Pharisees. Jesus' disciples "go on eating and drinking" while the others "often fast and pray." If a disciple's piety is a measure of the teacher, then why does Jesus seem unconcerned to encourage strict religious practices among his followers?

10. How does Jesus describe his mission in verses 31-32? As a doctor, come to help those who are "sick"—those who are sinful, and who know it. But those who think they are healthy ("righteous") will not go to the doctor and will not listen to him.

When you go to the doctor, you know you are sick and you know you need help. That's the kind of person that Jesus is calling; that's the kind of person who is willing to leave what he has and follow after him. That's the kind of person who winds up as a friend of Jesus: the one who knows he is desperately sick with sin. **How have we seen him enacting this mission in his words and actions from 4 v 14 to this point?** The self-confessed sinful fisherman, the leper, the paralyzed man and the tax collector are the sick people whom Jesus has come to treat—they are the sinners to whom Jesus has come to bring into his kingdom.

- **Who are the self-proclaimed "healthy" people in this section of the Gospel?** The two groups who don't understand Jesus and so reject him in this passage are the residents of his hometown, and the Pharisees. Both consider themselves "healthy." And the clear implication of Jesus' teaching is that the Pharisees aren't part of the equation. Jesus came to call sinners, not the righteous. That is to say, he did not come for people like the Pharisees.

EXPLORE MORE
[Fasting was a sign of mourning and/ or hopeful dissatisfaction with the present.] So, as Jesus' short story in 5 v 34-35 shows, why does it not make sense for Jesus' followers to fast? Jesus draws on an Old Testament image to help us understand what he means. He is like a bridegroom (this is a common Old Testament description for the relationship between God and his people; for instance, Hosea 2 v 19-20 and Isaiah 62 v 5). As long as Jesus is with them, his disciples (the "friends of the bridegroom") should celebrate. Now is not the time for mourning and hopeful anticipation. Fasting will be appropriate after Jesus is "taken from them" at his crucifixion and ascension, for at that time Jesus' followers will once again be in a period of anticipation, this time of his return. **Jesus' arrival has changed everything. How does his image in Luke 5 v 36-38 reinforce this?** Judaism is the old garment and the old skins. Jesus' coming and his ministry and his followers are the new garment and the new wine and new skins. Jesus hasn't come to patch up the things that were missing in Jewish religion, even in the religion of the very most pious people like the Pharisees.

Note: Verse 39 has presented a challenge for interpreters. Luke is the only Gospel writer who includes this saying, and at first glance it appears to be out of step with the message of the previous verses. In the little parable that Jesus has just told, his ministry is compared to new wine that cannot be contained by old wineskins, but in verse 39 it seems that it is old wine that is to be preferred. Two understandings suggest themselves. It could be that Jesus is offering an ironic criticism of the Pharisees and their rigid insistence on the religious forms that Jesus was making obsolete. In this reading, their love for "old wine" (which normally is the best wine) causes them to miss out on the really marvelous vintage. On the other hand, it could be that Jesus here is shifting his metaphor, acknowledging the reality that older wines are normally best. If this is the case, then Jesus is stressing that his coming is the true fulfillment and true meaning of the old-covenant religion that the Pharisees claimed to love so much .

Can you think of times when your expectations of following Jesus and his demands about following him have been different? Were you tempted to stick with what you knew and understood, rather than letting him change everything? It is easy to knock the Pharisees for their refusal to allow Jesus to change everything. But we all naturally cleave to what we know, understand, and are comfortable with. This question aims to help your group consider how they may have been tempted to react to Jesus as the Pharisees did. You may like to prepare your own answer to this, in case others cannot think of an instance from their own lives.

11. APPLY: Why, if you think of yourself as spiritually "healthy," will you not only misunderstand Jesus, but be angered or upset by Jesus? Those who are certain of their own health never go to the doctor; those who are confident of their own goodness and acceptance by God will never accept Jesus' offer of salvation. Not only this, but they will be offended at the suggestion that they need a cure, or that they cannot cure themselves. A self-righteous person is always angered by being told that they are a sinner who cannot do anything to save themselves. Sadly, it is easy even for followers of Jesus to become self-righteous (in some ways self-righteousness is the besetting sin of religious people).

12. APPLY: How does Peter (v 8-11) show us what it means to be someone who is spiritually ill, but who has been healed by Doctor Jesus? Encourage your group to compare/contrast their own response to Jesus with Peter's here:

- A deep understanding of our own sinfulness and our inability, left to ourselves, to stand in the presence of the Son of God.
- A grateful acceptance of his call to be part of his kingdom (sinful as we are).
- A consistent decision to be willing to leave anything and everything in order to live close to him.

Luke 6 v 1 – 7 v 50
4 HOW TO BE HAPPY

THE BIG IDEA
Real happiness lies in following Jesus, loving like Jesus, trusting Jesus, and appreciating our forgiveness.

SUMMARY
Note: This study takes in a lot of exciting passages that repay careful attention. You might choose to split this into two sessions; first, Q1-7, and then second, the Explore

More section followed by Q8-12.

Again, rejection and conflict are an ongoing theme in this section, especially in 6 v 1-11 and 7 v 36-50. Between those two episodes, Jesus chooses his apostles (6 v 12-16) and then delivers one of his most famous sermons, "The Sermon on the Plain" (v 17-49). This is a manifesto for Christian living—and it reveals that those who are truly "blessed' are not those who are wealthy or prized in the world's eyes. It calls Christians to love in the way their heavenly Father does; and it warns us not to seek mere behavioral change or verbal assent. (You will not have time in this study to focus on every aspect of Jesus' teaching—but do let your group discuss and apply those parts of it that particularly strike, encourage and challenge them.)

Jesus is revealing himself to be a surprising Messiah—even John becomes concerned about Jesus' identity (7 v 18-28). But Jesus, through his actions (v 1-17, 36-50), shows that he is indeed the King God had promised—but he has come in salvation to bring sinners into his kingdom, enjoying forgiveness, rather than in judgment. These themes are collected together in v 36-50, where Jesus confuses his host, a Pharisee, by forgiving a notoriously sinful woman—a woman who loves him much because she understands she has been forgiven much. Luke's challenge to his readers is to see ourselves as the woman, and not as the host.

OPTIONAL EXTRA

Discuss what happiness actually is, having watched these people struggle to come up with a definition for what it is and where it is to be found: youtube.com/ watch?v=g5ehWotcoqM (or search for "VOXPOP2 - What is Happiness?")

GUIDANCE FOR QUESTIONS

1. If you asked 10 people who live near you, "Where is real happiness to be found?" what kinds of answers do you think you would get? There is, of course, no wrong answer to this. And there are many possible answers. Encourage your group not to seek to come up with a "right answer," or to feel the need to criticize the answers their neighbors might give.

- **How would *you* answer that question?** Again, don't make your group seek the "right answer." You could return to this question after Q3 (which is Jesus' answer to the question) or at the end.

2. Fundamentally, these verses are about the distinction between two kinds of people. How does Jesus describe those types (v 20-23 and v 24-26)? The first group is "blessed," or happy—they are in the best position possible. They identify with the Son of Man (v 22) and the ancient prophets. And yet these people are poor, hungry, weeping and hated.

The second group is the recipient of a declaration of woe (so common in the ministry of the prophets—see, for instance, Isaiah 5 v 18)—they are in a terrible position. They are identified with the false prophets (Luke 6 v 26). Yet these people are also rich, well fed, laughing, and well respected. **Note:** It is important not to read Jesus' words in a flat sense: surely he is not declaring that every single poor person in the world is the recipient of God's favor, whatever their character or way of life. Instead, we should see that a person's economic condition has the potential to help or to hinder them when it comes to having the spiritual characteristics that God values and blesses. Equally, there is no virtue in being hungry—but those who lack physical comforts in this life are most likely to turn to God's promise of help. And Jesus is not against laughter. But he is saying that those who are blessed—part of his people—will weep over their own persecution or the wicked state of the world. Conversely, those who delight in and laugh with a world in rebellion against God will find themselves weeping in the world to come (v 25).

- **Where does each group enjoy their "reward" (v 23-24)?** The first can anticipate a "great … reward in heaven" that will more than compensate them for their present sufferings (v 23). The second group have "already received" (v 24) all the good that is coming to them. They should expect no further rewards beyond those meager and temporary pleasures that they receive from their earthly wealth. Woe to them!

3. How is Jesus redefining what it means to be happy, or "blessed"? The

default state of the human heart is to treasure whatever comfort, prosperity, and ease is available in this life. That, it appears, is the key to happiness. People say "money can't buy happiness," but mostly we do not believe it.

Jesus redefines the means to happiness in two ways. First, he warns us that those who make themselves at home in this world will face disastrous consequences when the kingdom of God comes in its fullness. Any "happiness" will prove to be very short-lived. Second, he promises that those who find themselves deeply dissatisfied with this world, and who suffer for following him, are happy—they will be blessed in the end, in his eternal kingdom, and can know joy now because they know they have eternal blessing ahead.

4. What does it mean for a follower of

King Jesus to "love" (v 27-36)? In verses 27-28, we read an exhortation to "love your enemies," followed by three parallel exhortations that serve to fill out the theme of loving enemies: "do good to those who hate you, bless those who curse you, pray for those who mistreat you." Then Jesus gives four examples of what that love might look like when it is put into practice.

- v 29: "If someone slaps you on one cheek, turn to them the other also." Most likely what is in view here is not so much a punch to the jaw but rather, a personal insult delivered in a disrespectful backhand slap. Jesus is enjoining his followers not to fight for their own dignity in such situations, but to remain engaged and even vulnerable to further insults.

- v 29: "If someone takes your coat, do not withhold your shirt from them." The sense here is that the disciple is being robbed of his outer garment, but instead of defending himself, he is to not even protect himself from having his undergarment taken as well. The sense is very similar to the previous example: personal affronts are to be met with open-heartedness and even generosity.

- v 30: "Give to everyone who asks you and if anyone takes what belongs to you, do not demand it back"—these two are very similar. Those who would love as Christ commands must be ready to be self-sacrificially generous to those who ask for help and also to those who help themselves to their possessions. The scope of these commands is broad; remain generous and vulnerable to "everyone" and "anyone."

Note: It is unlikely that Jesus meant these to be implemented literally—it is fairly easy to think of scenarios where a literal implementation of these principles would be absurd and displeasing to God. For example, a woman who is being abused by her husband should not feel constrained to subject herself to that abuse in the name of "turning the other cheek." Or if a heroin addict asks for money to buy more drugs and thus further enslave himself to his addiction, Christ-like love would compel the Christian not to give it to him (even though a literal implementation of Jesus' words would seem to demand that very thing). Instead, it seems Jesus is speaking in extreme terms in order to make a serious point about the way his followers love. Even in the crucible of insult and wrong, Christian love should be generous, forbearing, patient, and gracious, treating others as we would wish to be treated (v 31). The distinctive fruit in the life of a follower of Christ is love for one's enemies (v 35).

- **When someone loves in this way, what are they demonstrating about their identity, and about whose example they are following (v 35b-36)?**
  - When someone loves like this, they "will be children of the Most High" (v 35). This is not meant to indicate that somehow our loving has the power to make us into God's children, but rather, that when we love like God, we demonstrate our identity as children of the Most High.
  - When someone loves like this, we are following God's example—he is "kind to the ungrateful and wicked" (v 35); he is merciful (v 36). God's love is distinctive in that he pursues and saves and sacrificially gives his Son, not for good people but for his enemies (see Romans 5 v 6-8).

5. What does Jesus warn us against in Luke 6 v 41-42? A hypocritical attitude, which is blind to our own faults, but quick to notice the faults of other Christians, and

to point them out. He warns us against speaking to someone about their own "speck" before we have honestly considered whether we have a "plank" in our own lives, and have taken action to remove it. Our gaze should be on our own failures before we ever look to the failures of others.

- **Does this mean that a Christian should not judge that someone else is living wrongly, and point it out to them? Why/why not?** No! Christians should not be indifferent to the sins of their brothers and sisters. Jesus assumes that we should remove the speck in our brother's eye (v 42)—a passionate commitment to the teaching of Jesus demands that we do so. And in fact, the Bible repeatedly commends rebuke and correction as a way to show love to someone (e.g. Matthew 18 v 15; Proverbs 28 v 23). But only someone who has been made merciful and patient by the merciful and patient grace of God, and who is serious about identifying and fighting their own sin, is properly positioned to help someone else deal with their sin.

- **How do verses 41-42 shape our understanding of what Jesus is (and is not) saying in verse 37?** Verse 37 is not the battle cry of tolerance that many imagine that it is. There are places in Scripture where Christians are commanded to exercise discernment regarding the behavior and doctrine of others (1 Corinthians 5 v 1-5; Galatians 1 v 6-9). So it cannot be that in commanding us "do not judge," Jesus intends for his followers never to evaluate ideas or behaviors negatively. He is telling his people that we are to be quick to forgive (which requires that we say that something is wrong, but we will forgive it); and that we use the "measure" of judgment that we would like used towards us—and we know that God calls our sin "sin," yet does not condemn us. We are to judge according to God's standards ("measure", Luke 6 v 38) and forgive in the same way ("measure") that God does.

6. How do you recognize what kind of tree you are looking at (v 43-45)? "Each tree is recognized by its own fruit" (v 44). If you see pears, you know that you are not dealing with a thornbush but with a pear tree. If you see grapes, you know that you are not dealing with a greenbrier shrub, but a grapevine. There is a direct connection between the quality of a tree and the quality of the fruit that it produces (v 43). **How about what kind of person?** By how we live. Our external behaviors (the words we speak, our thoughts and attitudes, our actions) will inevitably reveal the motivations and loves of our heart.

• **So where is Jesus saying that real change must always begin?** In the heart. You cannot make a tree into an apple tree by pinning apples onto it. We cannot simply seek to pin obedience to Jesus' commands onto our lives. Jesus' sermon is not a program of external behavior modification—those behaviors will only ever spring from a heart that is captivated by his compassion and forgiveness.

7. APPLY: Which aspect of Jesus' "Sermon on the Plain" do you find:
• **most liberating?**
• **most counter-cultural?**
• **most personally challenging?**
Give your group time to think on their own and write down their answers, before you discuss them. Most likely each member of your group will have been struck by different

verses, in different ways. As you share your answers, make sure that your group has understood the passage correctly, and that they are thinking about their hearts as well as or more than their conduct. But let the discussion go in the directions to which the Spirit is prompting your group through God's word.

EXPLORE MORE
Read Luke 7 v 1-17. In what unexpected place does Jesus find faith (v 1-10)? A Roman centurion. He has a "great faith" that Jesus has found nowhere among God's ancient people, Israel (v 9). On the surface, it would be hard to imagine someone less likely to send people to approach an itinerant Jewish rabbi in order to plead for help on his behalf.

How does Jesus show his power in verses 11-17? He brings a dead man back to life (v 14-15). Jesus is powerful even over death.

How do these two episodes reveal who God's people are, and what help God has come to give them?
• God's people are those who have faith—and, as we have been seeing, they are often not those we would expect, and they are often those we would not expect.
• God gives his people life beyond death. This life comes to the boy (obviously), but also to the widow. She was in dire straits; not only was she enduring the grief of loss, but as a childless widow in that society she would have no one to provide for her needs in her old age. All her hopes and security had died with her son. Jesus is effectively giving her her future back.

8. Which two people are confused about whether Jesus really is the promised Messiah and a true prophet (7 v 18-19, 39)? v 18-19: John; v 39: a Pharisee.

9. But what kind of Messiah is Jesus (v 21-22)? One who has come to heal the sick, give life to the dead, bring good news to the poor, and welcome in unlikely outsiders (as 7 v 1-17 shows us).

- **How are his actions and words toward the sinful woman in verses 48-50 consistent with his answer to John?** Here, once again, a very unlikely person is welcomed by the King of God's kingdom, and forgiven of her sins so she can enjoy loving him. That is what the Messiah has come to do. He will come in judgment; but first he has come in salvation.

10. Who grasps this [the truth that Jesus has come to forgive, not to condemn], and who does not (v 29-30, 37-39)?

- v 29-30: Tax collectors understand it, and acknowledge that this is God's way. But the religious leaders do not.
- v 37-39: The "woman … who lived a sinful life" grasps that Jesus offers welcome and forgiveness to those who are ready to acknowledge and mourn their sin (v 38); but the Pharisee does not, thinking that if Jesus really were a prophet, he'd never allow himself to be touched by such a woman (v 39).

11. What is the correct answer to Jesus' question in verses 41-42? (Hint: You can use verse 43 to check your answer!) Make sure your group understand the parable. Two men owe money to a moneylender, but neither can repay the loan. The only difference between them is the amount that they owe; one man owes 500 denarii, roughly a year and a half's wages, while the other owes only one tenth of that amount. When the debt is canceled, which will love him more? The answer is simple: the one who owed more.

- **So what is the key to loving Jesus more (v 47)?** Understanding the depth of our debt to him, and our complete inability ever to pay it back. Are we more aware of our good deeds and moral rectitude (as Simon the Pharisee was) than of our deep need for forgiveness (like this sinful woman)? When we are weak and fall into sin, does it drive us to Jesus for mercy, or merely into a resolution to try harder and do better next time? The example of the sinful woman encourages us to be aware of our sin, not in order to celebrate it but in order to celebrate how great the grace and forgiveness of God really is.

12. APPLY: How can we speak in ways that belittle or undermine our sinfulness? Why is that dangerous for Christians to do? Encourage your group to think of any ways in which they joke about sin, or excuse it to one another, or suggest or live as though it is not very important. The danger this passage shows us, of course, is that if we ever stop thinking of ourselves as sinners in need of forgiveness, we will soon stop truly loving Jesus.

- **What is the connection between knowing we have been forgiven greatly… loving Jesus increasingly… and living out his commands in the Sermon on the Plain?** This question sums up the study and puts its two halves together. Begin to grasp how much we have been forgiven, and we'll love Jesus more, and so we'll love to please him by obeying his commands (e.g. in the Sermon on the Plain), and will be motivated and empowered to love others like him, in the way that he loves us. And, as and when we fail to live out the Sermon on the Plain in our lives, we will be reminded of our sinfulness… and appreciate our forgiveness more… and love Jesus still more.

5 Luke 8 v 1-56
OF SOILS AND STORMS

THE BIG IDEA
We need to listen to Jesus in a way that sees us obey his word; and then we can enjoy a life where we need fear nothing, because we know that Jesus is powerful over all that threatens us, and is at work for us.

SUMMARY
Jesus is by now being followed by a large crowd (v 4). That context is important to understanding the so-called, and famous, "Parable of the Sower," for, despite the subject matter of the parable, Jesus is not concerned about agricultural techniques or harvesting strategies. Instead, he is concerned to make the crowds understand that his message demands a response from those who hear it. His warning in verse 18 is a good summary of the larger point: "Therefore consider carefully how you listen." That is the focus of the first half of this study.

In the second half, Luke transitions from the importance of listening to Jesus' teaching to focusing on Jesus' actions. Verses 22-56 consist of three dramatic stories, covering four of Jesus' miracles. They each emphasize Jesus' power and authority—over nature, over evil, over sickness and even over death. Each implicitly calls for a response. And each demonstrates that Jesus has come to replace fear with hope in him and awe of him, whenever he is welcomed.

OPTIONAL EXTRA
The first half of this passage is about differing ways to listen to the same thing. So prepare a recording of 10-15 different noises (e.g. some birdsong; a car horn;

a baby laughing; part of your national anthem; horses' hooves), and play it in the background as your group arrives and gathers and chats. Then ask them what noises they heard—chances are they will identify none or very few of them, because although they heard them they did not hear them. Then play the noises again, at the same volume as before, but having challenged your group to write down after the recording has finished all the different sounds they heard. They will "hear very differently than they did the first time! You could refer to this activity after or during Q2 (and perhaps actually do the activity after Q1, and before you read Luke 8 v 1-21).

GUIDANCE FOR QUESTIONS
1. Why do people fear things? When fear is rational, it is because in some way we are in the presence of something (or someone) that has the power to remove something we feel we need; and so we feel insecure. Don't let your group spend too long on fears such as spiders or the dark; aim to move on quickly to the kind of fears that keep people awake at night.

- **Is fear ever a good thing? Why/why not?** There is no "right answer" here (though we will return to this in Q10). Often fear is a bad thing—it makes us feel worse, it stops us sleeping or enjoying life, and in some senses it changes nothing. It can also cause us to lose out on opportunities or make unwise decisions. However, fear is good in the sense that some things are wise to fear. We should fear lions enough not to go into a lion enclosure in a zoo! We should fear our boss enough to work hard, not lie, etc. And fear can cause people to do great things, make wise choices, etc.

2. What do we need to do? To think carefully about how we listen to Jesus' words. **What different ways are there to "listen" to someone?** By definition, all your group are listening to Jesus, since you have just read Scripture. But this question encourages you to think about the different ways to listen. Q3 fills this out further—but we can listen and ignore what we hear; listen, consider and then reject what we hear; listen, agree, but do nothing; listen and put into practice what we hear; etc.

3. What do the four types of soil in verses 5-8 represent (v 11-15)?

1. The "path" (v 5): The path in a field would be hardened; nothing would grow there. The birds represent the devil, who "comes and takes away the word from their hearts" (v 12). This first soil describes people who hear the word of Jesus but are hardened to it. It never takes root in their lives but is immediately gone, bearing no fruit.

2. The "rocky ground" (v 6): this kind of soil represents people who "believe for a while, but in the time of testing they fall away" (v 13). With these types of people, there is apparent spiritual life in response to the proclamation of the word. They receive it with joy (v 13) and initially all appears well. But when trials arise in their lives, it becomes apparent that the spiritual life is superficial. Just as the scorching heat of summer comes and tests the depth of a plant's root system, so the difficulties of life will serve to reveal whether or not the roots of our faith run deep.

3. The "thorns" (v 7): This kind of soil

represents people who "hear, but … they do not mature" (v 14). The new growth of spiritual life finds itself in competition with "life's worries, riches and pleasures." Those worldly concerns choke the life out of the plant and prevent the seed from growing into a fruitful plant. Many would-be disciples have found themselves walking away from Jesus in order to pursue worldly wealth and the pleasures of this life.

4. The "good soil" (v 8): When the seed meets a "noble and good heart" (v 15)— a heart that hears the word, retains it, and perseveres in it—the result is an impressive and fruitful crop. This spectacular growth more than compensates for the disappointment of the other three soils. Reaping a crop "a hundred times more than was sown" (v 8) represents an extraordinary harvest.

• **How does this show us what listening well means?** We must listen with our hearts as well as with our ears. Listening well means that we actually live by what we hear from Jesus. We let his word go to work in our lives, and we believe that the crop in our own life will be huge as we do so.
After all, the crucial difference between the "soils" in Jesus' parable is what they do with what they hear. All four soils receive the seed/"hear the word." But the first three don't hear it rightly—they don't embrace it and put it into practice, so there is no product/crop in their lives.

EXPLORE MORE
What has been "given" to the disciples (v 10)? The "knowledge of the secrets of the kingdom of God" (v 10). Jesus was speaking the truth to them and giving them the power to comprehend it.
What purpose do the parables have for

those who have not been given this (v 10)? They serve as a barrier to the truth. At the end of verse 10, Jesus quotes from Isaiah 6 v 9, to the effect that there will be those who hear him (in a physical sense) but never truly hear him (in a spiritual sense). The sound of Jesus' words reaches their ears, but the beauty and power of Jesus' message never reaches their hearts. This kind of people hear Jesus' words, but they don't understand them.

How does this humble you as a Christian? Because we don't understand Jesus through our own intellectual ability or tenacity in trying to work the Bible out or by our moral goodness, etc. It is humbling to realize that only because God chose to give us understanding can we grasp who Jesus is and what he offers us. We cannot listen well without spiritual help.

How might it affect the way you speak to those who are not Christians? First, be unsurprised if they reject what we say. There are three types of soil in whom the word does not grow. Second, be encouraged to keep telling non-believers about Jesus. They may be good soil, by God's grace. Third, since they need God to reveal the "secret," we must pray. And fourth, it is good to encourage non-Christians who say, "I just don't get it" or "I wish I could believe like you do" to realize that they need spiritual help to listen well; they (and you) cannot do it alone. Encourage them to do as the disciples did in verse 9 and ask Jesus to give them clarity about what the Bible says.

4. Who does Jesus define as being part of his family (v 19-21)? There is a kind of family that is closer than a merely biological relationship. Those who don't merely hear the word, but also put it into practice are truly his disciples. Jesus' "people" are not related to him by blood but by obedience to

his message.

• **How does this motivate us to listen well?** Jesus is inviting us into his family! In first-century Middle-Eastern culture, family was all-important; ties of kinship required family members to stand together, defend one another's honor, and so on. Jesus is offering to be that family member for us, if we will have an attitude of listening to him in a way that responds to his words obediently.

5. APPLY: What would it look like to be a member of your church, while also being:
• **path-like ground?**
• **rocky ground?**
• **thorny ground?**
Think specifically here about the ways your own culture, and your church culture, can encourage or excuse, or enable someone to hide, the three reactions that Jesus warns us against. After all, Jesus does not merely aim to inform us here, as if it were enough that we understand why it is that some people reject the word while others embrace it. Instead, Jesus is alerting the his hearers to the eternal significance of the way that we hear his word—and the possibility that we will not hear it well, and savingly.

• **Which type would you be most likely to become without even noticing?** Again, an opportunity to think hard about the ways in which we ourselves might most easily be duped into thinking we are listening well, when in fact the seed is not growing well in our hearts and lives.

6. For each episode, sum up who Jesus helps, and how, in a sentence: Obviously, your group members will each write something different down. Here are some examples:

- **v 22-25:** With a few words, Jesus helps his disciples, some of them experienced fishermen, by calming a storm that they thought would drown them.

- **v 26-39:** Jesus helps a man possessed by a legion of demons, by sending the demons into a group of pigs, so that he can be restored to his right mind.

- **v 40-56 (you can take two sentences for this one!):** Jesus helps a woman who suffered from untreatable bleeding, by healing her instantly; and he helps a man whose daughter is dying and then dies while he is on his way, by commanding her to stand up alive, which she does.

7. How does each episode show us people (or a person) in a "storm," literal or otherwise?

- The disciples are in a literal storm—one that threatens to end their lives. The panicked reaction of seasoned fishermen indicates that the situation at the beginning of verse 24 truly was dire.

- The man in the next episode is the most vivid and pathetic person we have yet met in the Gospel. He is entirely removed from life; he cannot live in the town, or be near others (v 27, 29). He is literally hopeless, with no hope of help.

- The woman's condition, apart from being painful and weakening, meant she was an outcast from society. Because of her bleeding, she was ceremonially unclean (see Leviticus 15 v 25) and would pass her uncleanness on to anyone who touched her. If she was a young woman, then this condition may very well have prevented her from having children, a particularly isolating condition in that society.

- The man stands to lose his daughter. He may be a synagogue leader, an important and respected leader, but death and grief

are no respecters of social standing.

8. What does each reveal about the nature of Jesus' power? In one sense, the answer is very simple—but encourage your group to recognize the awesome nature of Jesus' power. He has complete, instant and effortless control over nature, over evil, over illness, and over death.

⊻

- **Why is the disciples' question in Luke 8 v 25 a sensible one?** Because they have just seen a man calm a storm with a command. The question of who he really is is a natural one to ask.

- **Read Psalm 135 v 6-7. How do the disciples' words in the rest of Luke 8 v 25 answer their question?** Jesus is "the LORD"—God himself. Only he has this kind of control over the creation, to do "whatever pleases him."

- **What is the only moment in these three episodes where Jesus' identity is fully recognized?** In Luke 9 v 28, the question is answered by an unlikely source: the legion of demons tyrannizing this man recognize Jesus as "the Son of the Most High God." It will take the disciples until 9 v 20 to catch up!

9. Who is (or appears to be) afraid, and why (8 v 24, 25, 28-29, 36-37, 47-48. 49-50)?

- v 24: The disciples fear being drowned.
- v 25: The disciples are afraid as they begin to realize that there is only one category big enough for Jesus—he is God.
- v 28-29: The demons seem terrified of Jesus. They clearly recognize that he has complete power over them.
- v 36-37: When those who knew the demon-possessed man come to see

what has happened to him, instead of responding with gratitude and worship, they ask Jesus to leave because "they were overcome with fear." They seem to be terrified of having someone with such power anywhere near them. They had gotten used to having Legion around; the prospect of the One who can command those demons terrifies them.

- v 47-48: The woman is trembling as she approaches Jesus. It seems she just wanted to get healed and creep off, rather than having an actual encounter with Jesus. But Jesus won't let her slip away quietly.
- v 49-50: Jesus' words to Jairus in verse 50 show that Jairus is (understandably) "afraid": his daughter has just died.

- **Which fears does Jesus remove? Which does he not?**
  - v 24: Jesus calms the storm, removing the cause of his disciples' fear.
  - v 25: Yet he has in effect replaced that fear with a greater one: the fear about who he really is.
  - v 28-29: Jesus removes the fear from, and of, this man.
  - v 36-37: In one sense Jesus removes the fear—but he does it by removing himself from their region. Better to fear Jesus and enjoy his presence and power than have him leave.
  - v 47-48: Imagine how her heart must have leapt when the first word out of Jesus' mouth was a gentle "Daughter"! Jesus was looking for her so that he could correct her misunderstanding of what had happened. She might have thought that she was healed by touching Jesus' cloak, as if by magic. But Jesus wants her to know that it was actually her faith that healed her. He wants her to realize that she has no need to be afraid in his presence.
  - v 49-50: Jesus tells Jairus not to fear, but

to believe. Trust in him is the opposite of and antidote to fear of anyone or anything (other than a right fear of his power). And then he shows that it is wise to believe instead of fearing, by raising the girl from the dead.

10. APPLY: What do these three episodes teach us to do when we are afraid? Jesus' bearing and actions invite us to come to him in faith when we are consumed with suffering or fear; he is powerful and he is kind. He has come to bring an end to our fear, in his own way and in his own timing (the storm continued while he slept; the girl grew so ill that she died before he raised her). He is powerful enough to help us, and he welcomes us to come to him in our time of need. And whatever we fear losing, we need never fear losing him.

- **Is fear ever a good thing? Why/why not?** It depends what, or who, we fear—and what that fear causes us to do. We are right to be in awe of Jesus, who holds everything in his hands. We should, in this sense, "fear" him—and it should drive us to worship him but never to ask him to leave. We should not fear anything else—to do so is to doubt either Jesus' power to help, or his ability to do what he knows is best for us as his people.

11. APPLY: How do these episodes teach us to encourage others when they are facing storms? Encourage your group to think through what they naturally say to others when they are going through difficult times. Do they point them to the Lord Jesus? How can they do so in a way that does not sound unfeeling, but is clear?

6

Luke 9 v 1-62
FOLLOWING THE KING

THE BIG IDEA

The majestic, all-powerful, crucified and risen King Jesus invites us to follow him to his eternal kingdom, and to be involved in the work of the kingdom in this life. This is harder than any other life, but also more privileged.

SUMMARY

Up until this point, Jesus' mission has largely been a solitary one. But now a change is ushered in as Jesus summons "the Twelve" (9 v 1) and sends them out (v 2) with a two-fold mission that mirrors Jesus' own actions up to this point: "to proclaim the kingdom of God and to heal the sick" (v 2, 6). The one-man show just became a group enterprise, and this continues in the miracle of the feeding of the 5,000, where Jesus enables his disciples to provide what the people need (v 10-17).

In the middle of these two episodes, King Herod wonders who this Jesus is (v 9); and in verse 20, we find the first person to recognize who he is—God's Messiah.

We might expect this to be a triumphant celebration. Instead, Jesus unveils a shocking plan (v 22)—he must die (which is presumably why he asked his disciples to keep his identity quiet, v 21). Jesus makes it abundantly clear in the next verses that his messianic ministry would not begin with political triumph and military conquest. Jesus is God's Messiah, but the path that he will travel is not one of quick glory, but of terrible suffering. And to follow him also means suffering before glory (v 23-26).

It is in this context that three of the disciples

are given a glimpse of Jesus' heavenly glory, reassured of Jesus' identity, and commanded by God to "listen to him" in the "transfiguration" (v 28-36). The rejected, crucified Jesus really is the majestic Son of God. The rest of the chapter focuses on what it will mean to follow Jesus as he sets out for Jerusalem (v 51) and his death; and reveals to us what it will mean for us to follow the King in our lives today. It will be hard. It will be costly. And it will be a wonderful privilege, working for him in building his kingdom and ending in glory with him.

OPTIONAL EXTRA

Ask each member of your group to write a paragraph describing their dream job. Then shuffle them up, redistribute them among the group, read them out, and guess whose dream job is whose. Refer back to this in terms of the "job description" of following Jesus in this study—which is both a harder job and more wonderful than anything your group are likely to have written down for this activity!

GUIDANCE FOR QUESTIONS

1. If you could have any job in the world, what would it be? Why? There is no need for this to be a serious discussion. Let your group dream dreams!

2. What job does Jesus invite his disciples to share with him (v 1-2)? His mission. Jesus sends them on a two-fold mission that mirrors his own actions up to this point: to drive out demons and heal diseases; and to proclaim the kingdom.

The one-man show just became a group enterprise.

3. What job does he command his disciples to do in verse 13? To give the crowds (numbering 5,000, or possibly even more, since verse 14 only talks about "men") "something to eat." **What is the problem with the command?** They only have five loaves and two fish, which would not make a dent in the hunger of five thousand men! And the cost of buying food for that many people would be prohibitive. In other words, Jesus is telling his disciples to do something that is impossible for them to do.

• **How does Jesus make it possible for his disciples to do this job (v 16-17)?** Jesus himself miraculously provides the bread (v 16). Jesus gives thanks for the bread and then gives it to the disciples to distribute among the people—and, miraculously, it proves to be enough. They minister to the people but only because Jesus has given them everything they need to do so.

4. What is Peter's answer to the question, "Who is this" (v 20)? "God's Messiah."

• **Read 2 Samuel 7 v 12-13; Psalm 2; Jeremiah 23 v 5-6. By answering Jesus' question as he does, what exactly is saying about who Jesus is?** "Messiah" is a Hebrew word that simply means "anointed." In the Old Testament kings were anointed for the tasks to which they were called. And God had promised that he would one day send an heir of David who would sit on his throne and rule in a greater kingdom than his ancestor had known (2 Samuel 7 v 12-13). He would rule wisely and for the good of his people

(Jeremiah 23 v 5-6). And he would be all-powerful—while he would be opposed, his power would smash his enemies (Psalm 2). He would be the One God would raise up to rule his people in supreme power. Peter is saying that his friend Jesus is this figure—that he is the long-awaited, anointed ruler. There could be no higher, more mighty title that he could give Jesus. Don't let your group underestimate the size of the claim Peter is making (and that Jesus does not disagree with).

5. APPLY: What have these verses taught us about the work of Christian ministry? Of course, neither the mission in 9 v 1-6, nor the feeding of v 10-17, is a one-size-fits-all description of our ministry as Christians today. But these accounts do contain patterns and principles that still hold true now.
• Ministry is a job that is given to us by Jesus (v 1).
• Ministry is about showing the nature of the kingdom and sharing the news of the kingdom (v 2).
• In ministry, we need to be continually aware of our need and dependence; we must act out of faith in Jesus, and not our worldly provision (v 3).
• Ministry will not always be welcomed or popular (v 5).
• Ministry is about being invited to do what Jesus could do himself, but graciously involves us in and gives us the resources for (v 13-17).

• **Why do Christians have a privileged job? To what extent do you view this job as a privilege?** Every Christian has a ministry, a role among God's people given to us by King Jesus. And each is a privilege—it is something Jesus could do himself, but has chosen to do through you, and equip you for. And, since this is kingdom work, and since Jesus is the Messiah and his kingdom is eternal, this is work of the highest possible significance—work that will matter forever. There can be no more privileged job than working for this King. Discuss with your group whether you see it like that, and if not why not. Likely, our view of whether or not our ministry is a privilege is more influenced by the world's ideas of what a "good job" is than it is by the Bible's view of it.

6. What is shocking about verse 22?

Jesus is going to suffer greatly, be rejected, and die. This is God's Messiah, but the path that he will travel is not one of quick glory, but of terrible suffering. The paradoxes are stark: Jesus is talking about the Messiah and the Son of Man (both titles that connote glory and power) in terms of the Suffering Servant of Isaiah (see Isaiah 52 v 13 – 53 v 12). The most glorious One will suffer greatly and then be rejected and killed, not by the enemies of Israel but by its leadership. And this "must" happen—it will not be an accident or a result of failure, but as part of his Father's decree.

7. What will life as a subject of the Messiah be like (v 23)? What do these phrases mean for everyday life? Pick out

the two key phrases in verse 23:

Deny themselves: This is not about denying ourselves a frivolous purchase or declining dessert. This is about denying ourselves—giving up our supposed right to live the way we want to. Any attempt at discipleship that does not involve renouncing autonomy and self-love is not actually following Jesus in any meaningful way. If we would make him our master, we must first remove ourselves from that position. And this is a daily way of life.

Take up their cross: A man who was carrying his cross was on a one-way trip to

death. Jesus is not talking about physical death, though it's possible that following Jesus in this radical way could cost you your life. Instead, Jesus is talking about dying to your old way of life and crucifying the old, self-centered way of living. Following Jesus is like a kind of death because every area of a disciple's life is radically changed: our finances, ambitions, sexuality, entertainments, and relationships must all be brought into conformity with the wishes of Jesus. As a follower of Jesus makes the daily choice to pick up his cross, every part of that day will be impacted.

- **Why is it worth it (v 24-26)?** Because losing one's life is actually the path to blessing. If someone wants to "save" his life by refusing to pick up the cross of discipleship and by clinging desperately to his rights and privileges, he will find in the end that he has lost it (v 24). Whatever he has gained in the process of clinging tightly to his life will be lost in the end; even if he gains the entire world along the way, what good will that do him (v 25)? Paradoxically, the call to pick up your cross is a call to come and save your life. And Jesus warns that if a would-be disciple is ashamed of him and his words and will not confess him publicly, Jesus himself will be ashamed of him when he returns in judgment (v 26—see 12 v 8 for the same principle stated positively). If we deny our relationship to Jesus before men, he will deny that we are his on the last day. So following Jesus is the only way to save our lives and enjoy eternity, even though it requires us to give up our lives each day in the present.

8. Given what the disciples have heard in 9 v 21-26, why are verses 29 and 35 very significant?

- *v 29:* Here is confirmation that Jesus is

the all-powerful, glorious Messiah. He would suffer and die on the cross; but that did not mean that he is not the ruling, heavenly King.

- *v 35:* The cloud is a sign of God's presence, just as it was in the Old Testament (see Exodus 40 v 34-35). And so here God is confirming that the man who has just announced his own rejection and execution, and who has called his followers to deny themselves every day and give up everything every day, is his chosen Son. What do we need to do? Listen to him. Yes, Jesus' words about the nature of his kingdom can be unsettling. He is going to the cross and he calls his followers to pick up their crosses as well (Luke 9 v 23). But we need to resist the urge to soft-pedal these statements or ignore them. We need to listen to him. He is God's chosen Son.

EXPLORE MORE
Literally, the word translated "departure" in verse 31 is "exodus." With whom does Jesus talk about his "exodus" (v 31)? Moses—who had led the first exodus—and Elijah.
Read Exodus 12 v 21-32. When Israel were in slavery in Egypt under the power of Pharaoh, what plague did God send (v 29-30)? The death of the firstborn. In a single night, the firstborn son of every household would die.
How did Israel escape this judgment (v 21-23)? By taking a lamb, killing it, and putting the blood around their doorframe. Notice that Israel's families faced the judgment of God as much as Egypt's; they needed to trust in God's rescue plan of a lamb dying in place of their firstborn.
What did this achieve (v 31-32)? Pharaoh, who had previously refused to allow Israel to leave slavery under his hand, told Moses and

the people to go.
Moses, Elijah and Jesus think of the events Jesus will face in Jerusalem—his rejection, death and resurrection—as his "exodus." How does this help us understand why God's plan was for his Messiah to die in this way? In the first exodus, God provided a lamb whose death in the place of the firstborn son secured his life, and secured God's people's freedom. Now in this better, cosmic exodus, God is providing his Son, whose death in the place of his people will secure their eternal life and freedom. The first exodus was only a picture, albeit a wonderful one, of this greater rescue act of God's.

9. [Jesus will be killed, and it will take place in Jerusalem.] So how is Luke 9 v 51 a turning point in the Gospel? The time for Jesus to "be taken up to heaven" (that is, to die, rise and ascend to glory) was approaching, and so Jesus "resolutely set out for Jerusalem." **What is Jesus now deliberately walking toward?** His death. Every step closer to Jerusalem was a step closer to the cross.

10. What lessons about following Jesus do we get in this section? If you are short of time, split your group into pairs; ask them to look at one or two of these sections, and then report back to the whole group.

- **v 46-48:** Real greatness—greatness in Jesus' kingdom—is about showing love to even the very least. Jesus is not saying there's something inherently great about children. His point is that it's easy to be kind to the rich and powerful, because they can bless you back. We want to be perceived as great by others. Jesus says following him is about humbly blessing the lowly. Notice that Jesus does not attack the human impulse to achieve greatness.

Instead he redefines it.

- **v 49-50:** In the sense of doing ministry, those who are for Jesus are for him—even if they are not part of our group or do not belong to our tribe. We are to focus on following Jesus and doing our ministry for him, rather than on stopping others who also love him and wish to serve him (but are not quite like us).

- **v 52-56 (see 9 v 5):** James and John wish to call down heavenly fire on a village that won't recognize Jesus. But following Jesus is not about calling down judgment, but about offering salvation. Jesus has come to save those who reject him by dying in their place (a fact that is driven home by Luke in the book of Acts when the Samaritans become some of the first people to embrace the gospel—Acts 8 v 4-8, 25). The judgment is seen in Jesus and the disciples leaving (Luke 9 v 56—see 9 v 5). This is a warning of judgment—but it is not yet time for judgment. So for us—we carry the good news that Jesus offers God's salvation; we warn about judgment; but we leave the judgment up to God to bring, when he sees fit.

- **v 57-62:** Jesus warned these people he met on the road that membership in the kingdom must take precedence even over important social customs like performing burial rites for the dead (v 59-60) and other family obligations (v 61-62). There can be no compromise or half-heartedness. There is a cost to following Jesus, and it is often personally painful and culturally controversial.

11. APPLY: In which parts of your lives do you find it hardest to hear Jesus' words in v 22 and actually "listen to him"? Ask your group to be specific. Encourage them to write down some answers on their own before sharing.

12. APPLY: Why is following Jesus a wonderful "job"? Because, despite the hardships:
- we are following the Messiah.
- we can look forward to eternal life, knowing that whatever we "lose" now, we are saved forever.
- we will one day see Jesus in the glory that the three disciples glimpsed in verse 29.

7 Luke 10 v 1 – 11 v 36
YOU KNOW THE KINGDOM HAS COME

THE BIG IDEA

The main source of a Christian's joy is our membership of Jesus' kingdom. Ultimately, whatever else is true of someone, they are either under the joy-giving rule of King Jesus, or opposed to him.

SUMMARY

Jesus' disciples—this time, 72 of them—are once more sent to be part of his mission (10 v 1-16). When they return with understandable joy at the success of their ministry (v 17), Jesus gives them—and us—a lesson in where true joy must be found. "Rejoice that your names are written in heaven (v 20). Seasons of fruitfulness may come and go, and in any case the Lord will raise up other laborers after we are gone. We have a better source of joy; the promise of heaven has no peaks or valleys and the joy of belonging to the Lord knows no season.

And we experience this joy as we stay close to Jesus. Relating to him by listening to him is vital (v 38-42); and he teaches us how to speak to our Father in prayer (11 v 1-13). Blessing—joy—is found in obeying his word (v 28), because with the coming of the King, the kingdom has come and Satan has been defeated (v 20-22). So this study focuses on the characteristics of people who live in the kingdom Christ has brought: a joyful, obedient, listening and praying people.

OPTIONAL EXTRA

To introduce Q1, find pictures of various national costumes (e.g. costumes.

lovetoknow.com/National_Costumes_of_ the_World#4) and have your group guess which country each is from.

GUIDANCE FOR QUESTIONS

1. What are the main characteristics of people of your nationality, would you say?

• **Do you feel proud of your nationality? What difference does that make to how you live?**

Some people are very proud of being American, or Polish, or Ghanaian, and so on. For others, their nationality makes very little difference. Equally, some nations have well-known shared characteristics, although they are inevitably generalizations (English stiff upper lip; American can-do attitude; German efficiency; Italian passion).

You might like to return to this question after Q12 and consider how much our membership of Jesus' kingdom makes us joyful and changes our view of the world. You could point out that a Christian has more in common with another Christian who is completely different than them in every other way, than they do with someone from the same nation, or city, with the same hobbies and interests as them.

2. What does [Jesus] tell them they should pray (v 2)? This workforce is not nearly sufficient for the task of spreading the message, and so the disciples are encouraged to "ask the Lord of the harvest, therefore, to send out workers into his harvest field" (v 2).

- **What does he tell them they should expect (v 3)?** They are being sent out "like lambs among wolves." Wolves do not tend to treat lambs well. Just as their King will be rejected and ill-treated, so these disciples are not to be surprised if they face the same reaction.

- **What does he tell them they should proclaim (v 8-11)?** "The kingdom of God has come near." Notice how their acts of power are to give credence to the news that the kingdom of God has come near (and, in the person of the King, is about to arrive). And notice (v 11) that this message is preached as a warning to those who are rejecting them, as much as it is an invitation to those who are receiving them. Those who reject the message cannot say the kingdom did not "come near."

3. What warning does Jesus give the towns where he is sending these seventy-two followers (v 12-16)? That rejection will bring woe. Tyre and Sidon faced judgment in the Old Testament (e.g. Joel 3 v 4); but, Jesus says, if they had seen the kingdom come near in the way that Corazin, Bethsaida and Capernaum were seeing, they would have "repented long ago." Just as acceptance of the kingdom means salvation, so rejection of the kingdom brings judgment.

4. Why do the seventy-two return "with joy" (v 17)? Because "even the demons submit to us in your name." They had experienced an unanticipated provision of power.

- **Where does Jesus point them for their main source of joy (v 20-21)?** Jesus encourages their joy, but locates it on a different foundation: "Rejoice that your names are written in heaven" (v 20). They

should rejoice that God has revealed to them the reality of the kingdom, and the identity of its King (v 21). **Why does he do this, do you think?** Almost certainly, it is because their ministry has been so successful. It is a tremendous blessing to see the Lord working through you; growth in holiness and fruitfulness in ministry are good reasons to be thankful to God. But God has an even greater blessing for his people, for he has written their names in heaven. He has brought us into an unshakeable relationship with himself that will be fully realized in the joy of heaven. They need to learn not to put their hope in their service to God and the way that he may choose to use them. They may visibly be greatly used in one season, and not in another; but their place in heaven will not be affected, and neither should their joy be.

EXPLORE MORE
Jesus' famous story in v 30-36 is told in response to two questions an "expert in the law" asks him. What is the first, and how does he answer it (v 25-28)? "What must I do to inherit eternal life?" The wording of the question implies that he is looking for one discrete act that he can perform that will give him the key to eternal life. Jesus answers by asking the man to go to God's law (v 26). To inherit eternal life, a person must love God perfectly, and love their neighbor just as they love themselves. Jesus agrees—but it will soon become evident that the terms and scope of the commandment need to be defined carefully. **Why is the expert in the law not satisfied with this (v 29)?** Because he wants to "justify himself"—that is, to be in the right with God based on his own performance. So he seeks to clarify God's standards, asking for a limited definition of

who counts as "my neighbor." If eternal life requires him to love his neighbor, then how tightly can he draw the circle of people to whom he owes that kind of love?

How does Jesus' parable define who a "neighbor" is? Absolutely anyone, no matter how different than us they are, or traditionally opposed to us they are—and to love them means to imitate the Samaritan's extravagant, costly, self-sacrificing, culture-crossing love.

We usually read this parable assuming that we are to be the Good Samaritan. What happens if we read it thinking of ourselves, spiritually-speaking, as the man who is attacked? We actually bear more spiritual resemblance to the helpless man dying by the side of the road. We are in desperate need of someone to show love to us in our sin-sick condition. From that perspective, we can see that Jesus is the true Good Samaritan. He came to us while we were still his enemies; he met us when we were dead in our sins and trespasses. He paid the price so that our soul's wounds might be healed. Once we have understood that truth, we will find that we are able to truly extend ourselves in love to those in physical and spiritual need around us. A heart that has been touched by the unmerited love of Christ will be moved to show that love to others who may not deserve it.

5. APPLY: But what does this passage teach us about mission in terms of:

• **its urgency?** The harvest is plentiful—people are waiting to hear the news of the kingdom. But the workers are few. So we need to pray, but we also need to get on with it. For us, too, the King is on his way. The harvest needs to be brought in, and we are invited and commanded to do that.

• **its high stakes?** Verses 9-11: Acceptance of the kingdom message brings healing, blessing and salvation; rejection clarifies that someone is facing judgment.

• **what should bring us joy?** Primarily, what God has done for us—the truth that he has written our names in heaven and revealed the truth about his Son to us. Of course, it is a joy to be used by God. But seasons of fruitfulness will come and go, and in any case the Lord will raise up other laborers after we are gone. If our identity and happiness is wrapped up in those things, we will at times despair. But we have a better source of joy; the promise of heaven has no peaks or valleys and the joy of belonging to the Lord knows no season.

6. What is the "one thing" that will never be taken away from someone (10 v 38-42)? Investing time in listening to Jesus' teaching. Like any other relationship, a relationship with Jesus is based on spending time with him. Martha had forgotten this, and was running around seeking to serve Jesus, but spending no time with Jesus. We relate to Jesus not through our service, but through getting to know him through his word. And that relationship will endure through death, for we shall then see him face to face.

• **Why do Jesus' disciples, as they begin to be included in the work Jesus has come to do, need to remember this?** Because there is much to do for Jesus, and it is very easy for Jesus' followers to define their relationship with him in terms of "the preparations that [have] to be made" (v 40).

7. Jesus teaches his disciples the things that God loves to hear them pray about (11 v 2-4). What are they? Note that these are all requests—things God loves us to ask him to do:

- "Hallowed be your name" (v 2): a request that the name of God would be recognized and considered holy. In the Bible, a person's name includes his reputation and all that is said about him. God's name stands for all that he is, and so Jesus teaches us to pray that it would be hallowed.

- "Your kingdom come": imploring him to rule over us and every area of our lives, increasingly, so that his kingdom's purposes are accomplished in everything great and small.

- "Give us each day our daily bread" (v 3): we are to ask God for the things we require on a regular basis, because we are in need of God's provision daily. Think with your group about how Western lifestyles mean we tend to be less aware of our need than people were in Jesus' day. But a stocked pantry does not mean we are less dependent every day on God giving us what we need.

- "Forgive us our sins" (v 4): Jesus' followers are acutely aware of their failures and shortcomings (see 6 v 41), and so they know that they must appeal to God for forgiveness. It is perhaps a more subtle need, but we require this daily mercy from God every bit as much as we need him to give us our daily bread. And we ask him to enable us to forgive others in the same way as we know he has forgiven us.

- "Lead us not into temptation" (11 v 4): a petition for spiritual protection. Jesus is encouraging us to express an attitude that acknowledges that we need God's help and protection in times of temptation (1 Corinthians 10 v 13).

- **What does Jesus teach us about why prayer is wonderful (v 5-13)?** Don't linger over all the details here. Just pause to notice:

- v 5-10: God is ready to listen, and act, and give.

- v 11-13: God is our loving Father, and he knows what good gifts we need. He will always answer our prayers in the way that is best for us. And whatever else he gives us, he will always "give the Holy Spirit"—his presence, with us—"to those who ask him" (v 13).

8. When Jesus drives out a demon, what accusation is made about the nature of his kingdom (v 15)? That he is working for the devil (Beelzebul was a common name for the devil—it means "Lord of the flies" and comes from the name of a Canaanite god). By linking Jesus' power to the realm of demons and suggesting he is building Satan's dominion, his enemies seek to discredit that which they cannot deny.

9. What answer does Jesus give (v 17-18)? How does this prove that he is not working for Satan? Jesus bluntly points out the failure in their logic: "Any kingdom divided against itself will be ruined, and a house divided against itself will fall" (v 17). Satan is a murderer and destroyer; he loves to spread misery and suffering. Jesus, on the other hand, came healing and reviving. Given that, how exactly does it make any sense to attribute the actions of Jesus to demonic power? Why would Satan empower Jesus to fight against him? What ruler would divide his kingdom against itself (v 18)?

10. What *is* his work evidence of (v 20-22)? That the kingdom of God has come to this time and place (v 20). The illustration in verses 21-22 pictures Satan as being like a strong man with a lot of treasure, guarding his house without fear. People are like his "possessions"; they are enslaved to sin and oppressed by demons. As long as no one stronger than the devil comes along, they will never be delivered. But when someone stronger than the strongman comes and attacks, the treasures of his house can be liberated. That stronger man is now here.

11. What is the key application of Jesus' teaching here (v 28)? Spiritually speaking, the most important thing is that we hear the word of God and keep it. Signs and exorcisms may be exciting; trusting obedience to the King of God's kingdom is what counts.

- **From the passages we've looked at in this study, what does it look like to obey the word of God?**
  - 10 v 1-3: Seek to show and share the kingdom, and pray for others to join you.
  - 10 v 20: Find your greatest joy in knowing your name is written in heaven.
  - 10 v 36-37: Love your neighbor, as your Savior has loved you.
  - 10 v 42: Choose the one thing that is needed: whatever else you do, spend time listening to Jesus.
  - 11 v 1-4: Pray to your Father, and let the content of your prayers be pleasing to him.
  - 11 v 20: Recognise that Jesus has come to bring the kingdom of God.

EXPLORE MORE
The people had asked Jesus "for a sign from heaven" (v 16). In verse 29, he gets round to responding to the request. What is the only "sign" they will be given (v 29-30)? The sign of Jonah. He was a sign to the Ninevites (the inhabitants of Nineveh, where Jonah was sent to preach); Jesus is the same sign to his generation.
Read Jonah 1 v 15-17; 2 v 10 – 3 v 10 … What was the right response to

the "sign of Jonah" (Luke 11 v 32)? Repentance (see Jonah 3 v 3-10).
Why do the generation alive in Jesus' day therefore have no excuse for rejecting his message? Because "now something greater than Jonah is here" (Luke 11 v 32). Jesus is a greater preacher, since he is God's Son, and not merely a prophet. And where Jonah "only" went down to the belly of a fish for three days, and then was spat back to dry land, Jesus will really die, lie cold in a tomb, and then rise to new life. So if the Ninevites realized they must listen to Jonah on the basis of the "sign," there is absolutely no excuse for Jesus' generation not to listen.

12. APPLY: How do verses 14-26 show us that, when it comes to Jesus, there is no middle ground? When it comes to Jesus, there are no neutral people— "Whoever is not with me is against me, and whoever does not gather with me scatters" (v 23). Lots of choices in our lives are trivial and therefore unimportant, but when it comes to the Son of Man there cannot be a middle ground. Either he is the stronger man, who has come to bind Satan; or he is working by the power of Satan. If you are not for him, you are against him by default.

- **What implications are there for us in our view of the world, and our ambitions in this world?** We live our daily lives in enemy territory. The world does not share our loyalty to Christ and it does not care about the good of our soul; its default setting is animosity to the things of the Lord. While all people are made in God's image and are thus capable of doing all kinds of good things, their fundamental loyalties are different than ours. And so we must be prepared to walk cautiously in the world; and to proclaim the kingdom of God to the world.

8

Luke 11 v 37 – 12 v 34

FREED FROM WORRY

THE BIG IDEA

The God who will judge all people is our loving Father—so there is no need to worry about our religious performance (which leads to hypocrisy) or about our level of wealth (which leads to greed).

SUMMARY

Everyone worries by nature. Those focused on this world will worry about things such as their wealth and living standards—as the man who approached Jesus in 12 v 13-15 did. Jesus warned him about "greed." Equally, those who are concerned with the next life, and with deserving favor from God, will——like the Pharisees, end up living as hypocrites—focusing on externals in the hope that they can win the approval of others and of God. In this section, we find Jesus launching into a series of condemnations of such religious hypocrisy (11 v 39-52), pointing out to his disciples that it is ultimately fruitless, since God will reveal all things in judgment (12 v 1-3).

For Jesus' followers, there is no need to fear man (v 4), or fear not having what is needed. The only one worth fearing is God, who has power over eternity (v 5)—and he is our Father (v 32). The awfully holy God is more lovingly disposed toward us than we could ever fathom. That truth should set us free from the crippling fears that enslave those who do not know this God (v 30). He has set us free in order that we might seek his kingdom with our whole life (v 31) and then show the world how glorious and loving and trustworthy God is.

This is a fitting place to end these studies on Luke 1 – 12. The angels told the

shepherds there was no need to be afraid, for the Messiah had been born to bring joy (2 v 8-11). Here we find that Messiah telling his followers not to be afraid—and not to pursue wealth or hypocritical self-righteousness—because in him, they have a relationship with God that brings them forgiveness, current provision, and eternal riches.

OPTIONAL EXTRA

Before you begin, ask your group to write down their three biggest worries on separate slips of paper. After Q9 or 10, ask each individual to look at those worries, and write down any truths in this passage that have encouraged and/or challenged them in those worries; and then write down what it would look like to trust their heavenly Father with those issues in their life.

GUIDANCE FOR QUESTIONS

1. What do unreligious people worry about most, do you think? The aim here is to think about worries that are not connected to issues of faith or God. There are no wrong answers to this question, and probably no limit to the number of things people worry about. You could link back to this question immediately before or after Q5—money is a great worry for many people, whether they have it or not.

- **What about religious people?** This is a harder question to answer. But religious people (those who have a sense of a divine being whose favor matters greatly, and/or an eternity that their own actions can affect) will be anxious about their own goodness/performance. They also tend to care greatly how they compare to others, and how others think of them. This links to Q2—the Pharisees took their religious performance extremely seriously.

2. What surprises the Pharisee that Jesus is eating with (11 v 38)? Jesus' failure to wash his hands before eating. The issue at hand(!) is not hygiene, but rather the ceremonial washing that the Pharisees so cherished as a sign of ritual cleanness. These washing rituals were not required by the Old Testament law, but were a normal part of Jewish tradition.

3. What aspects of the religious approach of the Pharisees and the experts in the law does Jesus take issue with?
- **v 42:** Giving a tenth of their "mint, rue and all other kinds of garden herbs." The Old Testament law instructed the people of Israel to set aside a tenth of their produce in order to provide for both the priesthood and the financially vulnerable (Deuteronomy 14 v 28-29)—the Pharisees went over and above what the law required. On the face of it, this kind of tithing was a good thing, something that they were right not to neglect. But at the same time, they "neglect justice and the love of God" (Luke 11 v 42).
Make sure your group understand Jesus' point here (as with the rest of the "woes"). At first glance, the Pharisees' approach to their wealth seemed very godly; most pastors would be happy to have a church full of people who gave as liberally as the Pharisees. But good deeds done from impure motives result in "woe." They should have given their gifts from a heart compelled by love for God and a desire for justice.
- **v 43:** They love to sit in the most

important seats in the synagogues and enjoy the respect of the people as they walk around. This is what, at least in part, motivates their religious activity. The temptation to live for the approval and respect of other people is common to all people, but perhaps especially for those who are positioned as religious leaders.

- **v 44:** Explain to your group that because contact with a dead body would render a person unclean, graves had to be clearly marked so that people could avoid them. So here Jesus is comparing the Pharisees' corrupt spirituality to something repulsive and full of decay. But even worse than that, he is saying that they have the effect of making unclean those who wander into contact with them.

- **v 46:** God's law was meant to be a source of joy (e.g. Psalm 119 v 1-16), but the scribes had made it into something that paralyzed people with extra rules. Instead of helping people to understand and live out the blessings of the law, they did not lift a finger to help them.

- **v 47-51:** This is a complex woe! As the religious leadership of Jesus' generation reject him, they are showing that they are like their ancestors who killed the prophets. The leaders may have paid lip service to honoring the prophets in their day, but their failure to heed the message of the prophets showed that in reality they stood in solidarity with their ancestors who killed them. They are "held responsible" (Luke 11 v 51) because they stand in a long line of people who fundamentally reject those sent to them by the Lord.

- **v 52:** God's word was meant to be like a key that opened the door to a blessed relationship with him. But through their teaching, the scribes had made this key inaccessible. They did not use it themselves to enter into a walk with the Lord, and they even made it more difficult for those who were seeking to enter.

4. What one word does Jesus use to describe the problem with the Pharisees (12 v 1)? What does this word mean (the image in 11 v 39 helps)? Hypocrisy. They presented an external picture that did not match their internal reality. They polished the outside of the cup while the inside was filthy.

⊗

• **Why is religious hypocrisy dangerous to the hypocrite (11 v 42), and to those around them (12 v 1)?** It leads to "woe"—God's judgment—for the hypocrite. They look good, but have no saving relationship with God. And hypocrisy has the properties of yeast (12 v 1). Yeast spreads throughout a lump of dough and affects the whole. In the same way, religious hypocrisy has a tendency to recruit others into its charade. When we see others publically broadcasting their religious performance and their version of obeying God's law (whether or not it is genuine), it is easy to feel pressure to display a similar degree of accomplishment even if it is not backed up by an internal and private reality.

• **How far will this approach get them (12 v 2-3)?** Hypocrisy depends on the notion that we can hide the truth about ourselves. When someone professes to be godly but indulges their lusts or rage or greed in private, they are operating as if their public persona is the "real" version of themselves. Jesus explodes that foundation here. Every secret word and deed is open and exposed before the Lord, who judges

all (see v 5). Whatever our lips say, God knows what our hearts love. Whatever others see us do, God knows all our deeds. An awareness of that fact is a powerful antidote to the yeast of the Pharisees that threatens to spread in our heart.

EXPLORE MORE
… Read Isaiah 29 v 13; Hosea 6 v 1-6. How does God describe his problem with his people's attitude through these two prophets? Isaiah indicted Israel for their reliance on "human rules"; Hosea rebuked their reliance on religious rituals and the way their repentance and love were always fleeting, like mist.
What does God really want (Hosea 6 v 6)? Mercy toward others, and an acknowledgement of who God is and who they are, rather than merely external rituals.
If these prophets were around today, how might they find similar attitudes in our churches? Don't take too long on this question. One obvious answer is those who reduce their "Christianity" to attending enough meetings (Sunday services, prayer meeting, etc) at a good church; or to a checklist of a few particular commands (e.g. faithfulness to spouse, teaching children the Bible, giving a tenth away). Notice that all these things are good things in themselves; but they must never become the sum total of our Christian lives, nor the basis on which we think we are right with God.

5. What one word does Jesus use to describe the problem with the man's attitude (Luke 12 v 15)? Greed.

• **How does the parable he tells show how far this approach to life will get someone (v 16-21)?** Ask your group to rehearse the "plot" of the parable. A fertile field makes a rich man even richer. After some shrewd investments in infrastructure, he looks forward to sitting back and saying to himself, "You have plenty of grain laid up for many years. Take life easy; eat, drink and be merry" (v 19). But there is a catch, for that very night he is to die and give an account for his life (v 20). In the end, this man is a fool; he did not worry about the most important thing: being rich toward God (v 21). When it came time for him to give an account for his life, he was materially wealthy but spiritually destitute. His greed had brought him nowhere, except to judgment.

6. APPLY: What was the great aim of the Pharisees? To look good before God and before man. **What was the great aim of the man who asked Jesus the question in verse 13?** To secure greater wealth. He might have a legal case, but his aim is to have money, not to see justice done.

- **How do those aims in life look in your society (and perhaps in your church)?** This will vary from context to context. But both aims will be present.

- **Why do they provoke worry in people?** Relying on religious performance to impress God or others produces worry first because there is always a question about whether we have done "well enough" (and the correct answer is always "no"); it produces anxiety because of the gap between the inner reality and the outer show; and we are always at the mercy of others' approval and recognition for our sense of well-being.
Relying on wealth produces worry because we can always lose it! Further, it does not solve the problems and negate the worries that we thought it would (the cliché that money cannot buy happiness is a cliché because it is true).

7. What does Jesus tell his "friends" that they should worry about (v 5, 9-10)?
- v 5: the God who will give us the justice that we deserve for our sins: who "has authority to throw you into hell." You will one day die and face a God who has the absolute and final authority to send you to eternal punishment for your sins and misdeeds. We should fear God.
- v 9: the prospect of being disowned by God at judgment, because we disowned his Son in this life.
- v 10: blaspheming against the Spirit, which is unforgiveable. Much ink has been spilt trying arguing over the exact meaning of verse 10, and in the end it may be easier to say what Jesus does *not* mean by his statement. It cannot be that Jesus is teaching that there is a sin that too great to be covered by his atoning sacrifice (see 1 John 1 v 9-10). It also cannot be that God is unwilling to forgive someone who consciously chooses to reject Jesus (or else Peter could never be forgiven for his denial—see Luke 24 v 12). Instead, it seems best to understand what Jesus is saying as a way of warning us against a persistent rejection of the Spirit's witness to Jesus (referred to in 12 v 12). The Spirit witnesses to God's salvation in the person of Christ, then to obstinately judge that witness as false necessarily puts one outside of that salvation. Someone who desires forgiveness through faith in Jesus cannot be guilty of this sin.

8. But who are the people who do not need to fear this (v 8)? "Whoever publicly acknowledges me before others." If we have a right awe of Jesus, then we will love him, serve him, and remain loyal to him. (Note: We will also know that when we fail, we can turn to him in repentance and find forgiveness—v 10.)

9. Why else do God's people not need to worry?

- **v 11-12:** When we are called on to testify to Jesus in a hostile environment, we don't need to be anxious because the Spirit will help us (v 11-12). That doesn't necessarily mean that we won't be killed for our faith, but it does mean that God will help us testify truly and in so doing will preserve our souls.

- **v 24-28:** God cares for ravens (v 24) and clothes the flowers in the field (v 27-28), so how much more will he provide for all that his people need. The point is that we are infinitely more valuable to God than the birds (v 24), so we can trust his loving provision for us. In the end, if a powerful and loving God has declared his intention to make sure that his people are taken care of, there is nothing to be afraid of.

- **v 29-31:** God knows what we need. Those who do not know God are worried (v 30); that makes sense. But those who do know God know that he knows what we truly need, and will give it to us until he takes us to live with him; so it makes sense not to worry, but focus on living as part of his kingdom, and trust him.

- **v 32:** God's people know God is their Father, and Jesus is their Shepherd (they are his "little flock"). God loves us.

10. What is the sign that we have grasped that God is our Father as well as our judge (v 33-34)? We happily give up our wealth to provide for others, living in light of the realities of eternity. Our hearts are full of joy about our place in heaven, and invested in living for our lives there.

- **How is this approach to life the opposite to the approach of the man in the parable in v 16-20?** He lived for himself and his own comfort, so he used his wealth for himself (notice that the focus of his speech is always "I"). And he lived for the present. The Christian lives for God, and for his kingdom, so we use any wealth we have for others. We are living for our future eternal home.

11. APPLY: How does the gospel expose and undermine the need for:

- **hypocrisy?** The gospel confronts us with the fact of future judgment, and tells us we are sinful. But it also tells us that God loves us despite our sins and that his Son came to die for those sins. There is no need to hide them from him—in fact, as we "uncover" them before him and ask him to forgive them, he does so. We can be real about who we are, including our flaws. And enjoying his forgiveness and approval, we need not fear what others think of us. There is no need to wear a mask so that others think well of us.

- **greed?** The gospel confronts us with the fact that we will die and face judgment, and that we cannot take our wealth with us. But it also assures us of riches in our eternal home beyond anything we could grasp in this life. Knowing we are loved by God and on our way to his eternal glory frees us from any need to live for wealth now.

12. APPLY: Reflect on Luke 1 – 12. How has looking at the coming of God's King, and his kingdom: • excited you? • surprised you? • challenged you? • liberated you from fear?

This is an opportunity to reflect on the previous eight studies as a whole. Encourage your group to write down their own answers before sharing as a group. And members may wish to focus just on one or two of the questions here, rather than all four.

the good book

COMPANY

BIBLICAL | RELEVANT | ACCESSIBLE

At The Good Book Company, we are dedicated to helping Christians and local churches grow. We believe that God's growth process always starts with hearing clearly what he has said to us through his timeless word—the Bible.

Ever since we opened our doors in 1991, we have been striving to produce Bible-based resources that bring glory to God. We have grown to become an international provider of user-friendly resources to the Christian community, with believers of all backgrounds and denominations using our books, Bible studies, devotionals, evangelistic resources, and DVD-based courses.

We want to equip ordinary Christians to live for Christ day by day, and churches to grow in their knowledge of God, their love for one another, and the effectiveness of their outreach.

Call us for a discussion of your needs or visit one of our local websites for more information on the resources and services we provide.

Your friends at The Good Book Company

thegoodbook.com | thegoodbook.co.uk
thegoodbook.com.au | thegoodbook.co.nz
thegoodbook.co.in